▼▼▼▼▼▼▼▼▼▼▼▼▼▼▼▼▼▼▼▼▼▼▼▼▼▼▼▼▼▼▼▼

A Teacher's Guide to African Narratives

D1563023

SARA TALIS O'BRIEN

Rivier College

HEINEMANN
Portsmouth, NH

This book is dedicated to
the students and teachers of East Africa
and
OB

Heinemann
A division of Reed Elsevier Inc.
361 Hanover Street
Portsmouth, NH 03801–3912

Offices and agents throughout the world

Library of Congress Cataloging-in-Publication Data
O'Brien, Sara Talis.
    A teacher's guide to African narratives / Sara Talis O'Brien.
       p.   cm.
    Includes bibliographical references and index.
    Contents: Chinua Achebe and Things fall apart—Buchi Emecheta and The joys of motherhood—Okot p'Bitek and Song of Lawino and Song of Ocol—Ngugi wa Thiong'o and A grain of wheat—Bessie Head and When rain clouds gather—Alex La Guma and Time of the butcherbird.
    ISBN 0-325-00039-5 (Heinemann)
    1. African fiction—History and criticism. 2. African fiction—Study and teaching. I. Title.
PL8010.6.027   1998
809.3'0089'96—dc21
                                     98-9592
                                        CIP

Editor: Jim Lance
Production: Abigail M. Heim
Cover design: Jenny Jensen Greenleaf
Cover Art: Detail from a batik by an anonymous East African artist (collection of Sara Talis O'Brien). Design consultant: Theresa Couture, p.m.
Illustrations: Ann T. Ball
Maps: Daniel Marino
Manufacturing: Louise Richardson

Contents

▼▼▼▼▼▼▼▼▼▼▼▼

Acknowledgments

▼▼▼▼▼▼▼▼▼▼▼▼▼▼▼▼▼▼▼▼▼▼▼▼▼▼▼▼

I wish to thank Michael C. Kirwen for his encouragement and his influence upon me and Renee Schatteman for her careful reading of the manuscript.

Introduction

Few students in western nations of the world have had the opportunity to study the history of the vast continent of Africa, meet her people, and explore her cultures. Many are truly unaware that Egypt, an ancient civilization which developed a complex system of hieroglyphics and built massive pyramids commemorating the pharaohs, is in fact part of the great African continent. Likewise, the stories of leaders like Sundiata and Mansa Musa, who built the powerful Mali Empire of the Sahara and developed the Islamic center of learning at Timbuktu, are virtually unknown.

As literature provides a window on the world, *A Teacher's Guide to African Narratives* stands as an invitation to explore Africa through literature. This guide strives to assist high school teachers by synthesizing anthropological and historical material that is difficult to access, thereby providing a sound background for teaching texts that require knowledge of Africa. The guide reviews six African narratives that are written or translated into English, accessible in the United States, and appropriate for use in a variety of units on different reading levels. The novels and stories presented in this resource are selected from West, East, and southern Africa and introduce a variety of universal themes which raise complex issues. The narratives present the experience of particular ethnic groups in various regions of Africa, allow students to enter an African world, and analyze issues from another perspective. These narratives may be integrated into larger units on cultural diversity, literature, psychology, social studies, sociology, and women's studies; or the texts may be taught together as a semester's course focusing on the peoples, cultures, history, and literature of Africa.

Literature reflects the persistent and tenacious nature of culture, and tales passed on for generations in Africa form an extensive and pervasive base of knowledge and shared experience for particular ethnic groups. Modern African writers take inspiration from the oral traditions of their people and write in indigenous and European languages. These artists paint vivid descriptions of life in Africa, dramatize the profound effect of change, and in many cases chronicle the history of a particular ethnic group. The various peoples represented in this guide include the Igbo of Nigeria, the

Gikuyu of Kenya, the Acholi of Uganda, the Tswana of Botswana, and various ethnic groups of southern Africa.

The narratives highlighted in this text are arranged in a chronological progression. The first two authors, Chinua Achebe and Buchi Emecheta, write about the Igbo people of Nigeria. Chinua Achebe's seminal text *Things Fall Apart* describes precolonial Africa and illustrates how tension within traditional life erupts as the Igbo religion is defied and the people face the forces of British imperialism. In Emecheta's novel, *The Joys of Motherhood,* the protagonist Nnu Ego moves from the traditional Igbo world into the colonial world of Lagos. Through her difficult life of nurturing children, she learns that womanhood is not defined solely by motherhood.

The next two chapters focus on East African writers and continue the theme of clashing cultures introduced by the Nigerian writers. Okot p'Bitek's *Song of Lawino* and *Song of Ocol* illustrate the conflict of cultures through the biting satirical dialogue between husband and wife. In *Song of Lawino*, an Acholi woman begs her westernized husband Ocol to respect the traditional values of his people. Ocol responds by spurning his wife and all she represents as he attempts to build a new Uganda based on European models. Ngugi wa Thiong'o's *A Grain of Wheat* moves the conflict further into the realm of the psychological as it recounts the history of the Gikuyu people and celebrates the victory of the Mau Mau freedom fighters in Kenya. Ngugi illustrates the intense internal conflict caused by betrayal and recognizes the power of reconciliation within the revolutionary process; here, external and internal revolutions provide individuals with hope for true freedom from oppression.

The southern African writers continue the theme of revolution. *When Rain Clouds Gather*, by Bessie Head, illustrates the persistence and hope of the Tswana people of Botswana and the refugees they harbor. These ordinary people of different ethnic origins are determined to organize new, sustainable agricultural projects in a barren and rainless land. Finally, Alex La Guma's *Time of the Butcherbird* may be presented as reviewing the social history of South Africa as it retells the story of the interaction of ethnic groups. Here, the African people are called to organized resistance in order to eliminate the political ideology of apartheid.

Each chapter of this guide focuses on one author and begins with a brief discussion of some of the major issues raised by one particular text appropriate for students on the high school level. The basic plot of the text is presented along with pertinent historical information. This summary provides the rationale for teaching the work and is followed by a discussion of the literary techniques employed by the author and points for students to ponder. An anthropological or historical focus provides further background for understanding the narrative. For example, a study of the traditional Igbo title system provides insight to the protagonist's quest for status in *Things Fall Apart*; a reflection upon the traditional cycle of life illuminates the experience of the Mau Mau freedom fighters in *A Grain of Wheat*; and a review of land and labor issues in apartheid South Africa explains the forced removal of the African peoples in *Time of the Butcherbird*.

The second part of each chapter is devoted to the author. This section includes background information on the writer's life and summaries of the author's works. By understanding the writer's experience and the themes addressed in his or her oeuvre, teachers will be able to locate and present an African narrative in context with a certain level of confidence and authority. This background material will also assist teachers in selecting other texts for future courses or recommending narratives for students who are interested in independent reading. The final section includes an annotated bibliography of resources which may assist teachers in preparing new units and course syllabi.

In addition to the works reviewed in this guide, teachers may wish to consider texts more explicitly reflecting precolonial Africa as well as contemporary African literature of the 1980s and 1990s. Camara Laye's *The Dark Child* and D. T. Niane's translation of *Sundiata: An Epic of Old Mali* reflect various aspects of precolonial Africa. The emerging voices of African women like Sindiwe Magona of South Africa and Tsitsi Dangarembga of Zimbabwe also offer a fresh perspective on the situation of women in Africa and issues of colonialism. All of these works are suitable for students on lower or intermediate high school reading levels.

Camara Laye's beautiful short autobiographical piece, *The Dark Child*, is particularly appropriate for addressing the theme of growth from childhood to adulthood. This text specifically reflects the precolonial experience of a young boy in the Mandinka region of Guinea in West Africa. Camara leaves his homestead to attend a Koranic school and then travels hundreds of miles away to enroll in a French vocational school. Finally, he leaves Africa and his childhood experience behind for an education in Paris. The novel introduces students to Islamic influence in Africa and presents a lyrical, pristine image of the traditional African community working together—especially at harvest time. The individual's growth from childhood to adulthood is a process which is marked by the complex and profound initiation rite in West Africa and complicated by the introduction of formal western education.

D. T. Niane's translation of *Sundiata: An Epic of Old Mali* is another reflection of the precolonial experience in West Africa. The overall themes of this short epic focus on the destiny of the individual, the political complexities of emerging nations, and the value of cooperation. The narrative retells the oral traditions as sung by generations of professional praise poets and reflects the life of the Mandinka people in the thirteenth century. Students are introduced to Sundiata, a remarkable young boy who, as a child, is unable to walk. As the kingship passes to his enemies, Sundiata moves from court to court cultivating the cooperation of allies. He soon overcomes his disability and unites the twelve kingdoms of Mali into a powerful empire that stretches across the savannah from the Atlantic Ocean to Timbuktu. The empire of the great Lion King of Mali included the modern nations of Mali, Senegal, Guinea, Burkina Faso, and the Gambia.

In addition to these texts, teachers searching for more contemporary themes may wish to turn to emerging voices in southern African literature. *Living, Loving, and Lying Awake at Night*, published in 1991 by Sindiwe Magona, is an excellent collection of related short stories addressing the issues of maids, madams, and life in a divided South Africa. In the first section of the text, Atini leaves her children in the homeland to work as a maid in the city. Atini's friends, Stella, Sheila, Sophie, Virginia, Joyce, and Lillian, who also serve as maids to ensure their families' survival, all have their own dramatic stories. In the second section of the text, a variety of vignettes are presented which illustrate the humanity of the black South African people. Often, in order to illustrate the complexity of life in South Africa, the characters are presented in parallel situations juxtaposed to their white South African counterparts.

Tsitsi Dangarembga explores the complex quest of young women to secure a formal western education in colonial Rhodesia in *Nervous Conditions*, published in 1988. This outstanding work clearly contrasts the educational opportunities afforded young African men with those afforded young women like the narrator, Tambudzai. The novel also illustrates the neurotic condition of African youths like Nyasha, who becomes obsessed with the matriculation exam and becomes bulimic as she attempts to imitate the whites. The title of the novel springs from Jean-Paul Sartre's introduction to Frantz Fanon's *The Wretched of the Earth* and refers to the "nervous condition" introduced among African people by the European settlers. An analysis of this condition illustrates the deep psychological effects of colonization and the struggle of young African men and women to straddle two worlds.

The works presented in this guide are not an attempt to set a canon of African literature or review all the African authors and narratives suitable for study on the high school level. Teachers will find many other stories and novels from many other outstanding West African authors, including Flora Nwapa of Nigeria, Ousmane Sembene of Senegal, and Ama Ata Aidoo of Ghana, to be appropriate for high school students. Teachers may also wish to explore the short stories and poetry of East African writers such as Grace Ogot and Taban lo Liyong, as well as the narratives of southern African writers like Njabulo Ndebele, Doris Lessing, and Nadine Gordimer. It is my hope that this guide will introduce high school teachers to African literature and provide a sound background for teaching the texts reviewed.

Finally, as peoples of the world are becoming increasingly interconnected, more and more teachers are responding to demands to diversify the curriculum and foster global awareness. As a result of learning about peoples of various cultures, students gain a better understanding of the complicated international world around them and develop a sensitivity to the nature and complexity of ethnic diversity. By exploring African literature, I believe students and teachers will develop a profound respect for the people of Africa and be better equipped to function in a multicultural society. As literature provides a unique window through which we may see the world and other cultures, it also brings the dry bones of history to life. I hope *A Teacher's Guide to African Narratives* is helpful to high school teachers and contributes to this profound truth.

Resources

ACHEBE, CHINUA, with C. L. INNES, eds. *African Short Stories: Twenty Short Stories from Across the Continent*. Portsmouth, N.H.: Heinemann, 1985.

———. *The Heinemann Book of Contemporary African Short Stories*. Portsmouth, N.H.: Heinemann, 1992.

AIDOO, AMA ATA. *No Sweetness Here and Other Stories*. New York: The Feminist Press, 1995.

BRUNNER, CHARLOTTE H., ed. *The Heinemann Books of African Women's Writing*. Portsmouth, N.H.: Heinemann, 1993.

COURLANDER, HAROLD. *The Cow-Tail Switch and Other West African Stories*. First published in 1947. New York: Henry Holt, 1986.

———. *A Treasury of African Folklore: The Oral Literature, Traditions, Myths, Legends, Epics, Tales, Recollections, Wisdom, Sayings, and Humor of Africa*. New York: Crown Publishers, 1975.

DANGAREMBGA, TSITSI. *Nervous Conditions*. Seattle: Seal Publishers, 1989.

FANON, FRANTZ. *The Wretched of the Earth*. New York: Grove Press, 1963.

GORDIMER, NADINE. *Crimes of Conscience: Selected Short Stories*. London: Heinemann, 1991.

———. *A Soldier's Embrace*. London: Heinemann, 1980.

LAYE, CAMARA. *The Dark Child: The Autobiography of an African Boy*. First published in 1954 by Farrar, Straus, and Giroux. Translated from the French by James Kirkup and Ernest Jones. New York: Hill and Wang, 1991.

LO LIYONG, TABAN. *Eating Chiefs: Lwo Culture from Lolwe to Malkal Selected, Interpreted, and Transmuted by Taban lo Liyong*. London: Heinemann, 1970.

MAGONA, SINDIWE. *Living, Loving, and Lying Awake at Night*. New York: Interlink Books, 1991.

NDEBELE, NJABULO. *Fools and Other Stories*. New York: Readers International, 1986.

NIANE, D. T. Sundiata: *An Epic of Old Mali*. Translated by G. D. Pickett. First published by Presence Africaine in 1960. New York: Longman African Classic, 1986; reprinted 1987.

NWAPA, FLORA. *Efuru*. Portsmouth, N.H.: Heinemann, 1966.

P'BITEK, OKOT. *Hare and Hornbill*. London: Heinemann, 1978.

ROSENBERG, DONNA. *World Literature: An Anthology of Great Short Stories, Drama, and Poetry*. Lincolnwood, Ill.: National Textbook Co., 1992.

SCANLON, PAUL A., ed. *Stories from Central and Southern Africa*. London: Heinemann, 1989.

SCHEUB, HAROLD. *The African Storyteller: Stories From African Oral Traditions*. Dubuque, Iowa: Kendal/Hunt Publishing Co., 1990.

SEMBENE, OUSMANE. *God's Bits of Wood*. First published in 1960. Translated from the French by Francis Price and reprinted, London: Heinemann, 1989.

———. *Tribal Scars and Other Stories*. First published in 1962. Translated from the French in 1974 by Len Ortzen. London: Heinemann, 1987.

AFRICA

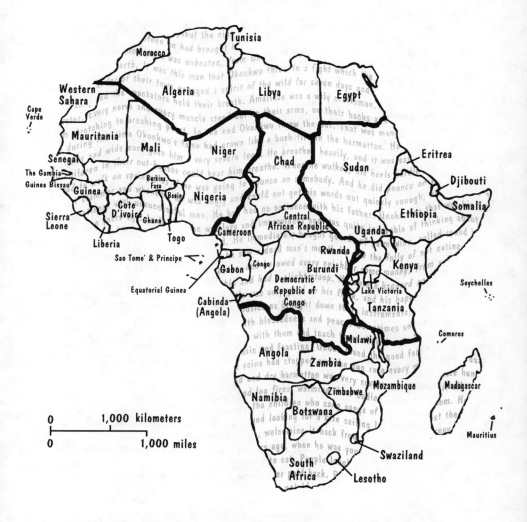

THIS MAP OF AFRICA HAS BEEN DIVIDED INTO NORTH, EAST, WEST, CENTRAL, AND SOUTHERN REGIONS.

Chapter 1

Chinua Achebe and Things Fall Apart

Chinua Achebe is internationally celebrated as one of the most influential African writers of the twentieth century. Translated into nearly thirty languages, his first novel, *Things Fall Apart*, has sold millions of copies and has been incorporated into the standard curriculum of many school systems throughout Africa, Europe, and North America. The novel, written in 1958, just before Nigeria gained independence, attempts to recreate the complex and diverse precolonial Igbo society in West Africa and dramatize the colonization of the Igbo by the British in the nineteenth century. The main issues raised by the novel focus on the conflict between European imperialism and the traditional value system of the Igbo people. Okonkwo, the protagonist, struggles to become great in the traditional world and refuses to submit to colonial forces. However, as the Europeans introduce Christianity, Okonkwo and the entire traditional Igbo society experience cataclysmic change.

Things Fall Apart is suitable for students on the lower or intermediate levels. This guide presents a basic overview of the novel and a brief history of the Igbo people living in areas along the Niger River. A review of the literary techniques, points for students to ponder, and an anthropological focus on traditional titles in Igbo society follows. Finally, an overview of the author's life and work is presented as well as an annotated list of resources.

Things Fall Apart and the Igbo People of Nigeria

Things Fall Apart, Achebe's first work, attempts to recreate the social, cultural, and religious fabric of traditional Igbo life between 1850 and the early 1900s. The novel depicts conflicts and tensions within Igbo society as well as changes introduced by colonial rule and a new Christian world view. These clashes result in societal upheaval that ultimately destroys the life of one man—Okonkwo, a talented but tragic Igbo who struggles to achieve success in the traditional world. The novel is structured in three parts: Part One depicts life in precolonial Igboland, Part Two relates the arrival of the Europeans, and Part Three recounts the beginning of systematic colonial control and the introduction of Christianity in eastern Nigeria.

As the novel begins, Okonkwo, a powerful man, is introduced as a great wrestler, a renowned warrior, and a hardworking member of the community. In addition to two barns filled with yams, Okonkwo has amassed three wives, many children, and two titles. His goal is to move through the traditional Igbo title-taking system—an intricate process which requires a balance of personal achievement and community service. However, although Okonkwo feels he is destined for greatness, his *chi*, or the god-force within him which controls his fate, is ambiguous. The outcome of his destiny is uncertain.

Because Okonkwo seeks to overpower his mediocre *chi* and is profoundly afraid of failure in life, he struggles to balance the feminine energy of life-giving love and the masculine energy of material success. Okonkwo often suppresses his feminine side as he pursues his goals, which angers the Earth Goddess Ani. His rage, his inflexibility, and his fear of appearing weak like his lazy father, Unoka, who has not earned any titles, consistently overshadow his respect for his family and community. For example, Okonkwo cares for his daughter, Ezinma, who is an *ogbanje*, or a changeling child who continually dies only to return to her mother's womb to be reborn and die again. He follows his second wife, Ekwefi, and the priestess Chielo to consult the oracle Agbala. He also locates and destroys the child's *iyi-uwa*, a sacred stone which links her with the spirit world. However, the humble father of this haunting journey has a dark and dangerous side, for he controls his family through anger. In bouts of rage, he takes a shot at Ekwefi and beats his youngest wife, Ojiugo, during a traditional celebration called the week of peace.

The same ambiguous pattern is illustrated by Okonkwo's relationship with his sons. Okonkwo respects his adopted son, Ikemefuna, the captive given to Umuofia by another village in order to avoid war. Okonkwo seems to admire Ikemefuna, for within himself the youth successfully balances the feminine and masculine principles as both a talented musician and a great hunter. The youth also becomes a brother and role model for Okonkwo's eldest son, Nwoye, who appears to be lazy. Yet fear destroys Okonkwo's relationship with his sons. When the Earth Goddess Ani commands the ritual killing of Ikemefuna, Okonkwo is warned by Ezeudu, the eldest member of the community, not to participate in the sacrifice. However, blinded by his fear of appearing weak, Okonkwo ignores the warning and deals the final death blow to Ikemefuna. Okonkwo's action ultimately shatters Okonkwo's relationship with his sensitive son Nwoye.

Okonkwo's actions also affect his community. During the funeral rite for the elder Ezeudu, Okonkwo's gun accidentally explodes, killing Ezeudu's son. Okonkwo's crimes enrage the Earth Goddess Ani, for he has consciously and unconsciously chosen death. His irrational actions are destroying the moral fabric of traditional life. Therefore, Ani banishes Okonkwo to his mother's village for seven years.

The setting of Part One of the novel is Umuofia, a union of nine villages. Although political organizations and beliefs differed throughout Igbo territory, in many ways, Umuofia reflects the typical independent Igbo villages that interacted with other villages in clusters. Historically, a common Igbo village was a direct democracy bound to a group of many villages by the decisions of a general assembly. The local life of each village was shaped by age-grade associations, title-making societies, work associations, religious fraternities, and secret societies. In many cases, the village was a democracy where men and women attempted to achieve prestige and status by accumulating wealth with which they purchased titles. These title-holding leaders influenced the village assembly, came to decisions through consensus, made new laws, and administered justice. These leaders were responsible for community service.

In addition to the social and political systems of the people, Part One of the novel reflects the complex religious tradition of the Igbo. In this world view, the creator god Chukwu is a remote masculine force. Chukwu taught the people to survive through the cultivation of yams, and the yam stood as an indicator of wealth and a type of currency within the society. The masculine Chukwu is balanced by the Earth Goddess Ani, or Mother Nature. The feminine Ani is closer to humankind than Chukwu, for she functions as the goddess of fertility and the arbitrator of morality; it is Ani who punishes those who destroy life.

In the traditional Igbo world view, these great masculine and feminine creative forces were augmented by localized deities, spirits, and oracles institutionalized by various Igbo communities. Each oracle spoke through a priest or priestess and served as a medium through which divine will was understood. The Igbo further personified the power of God in the concept of the *chi*, the personalized god-force or invisible power of fate which guided each individual through life. It was the finely-tuned *chi* that simultaneously controlled a person's fortunes in life yet allowed the individual free will to work creatively toward success or failure.

Part Two of *Things Fall Apart* takes place while Okonkwo is in exile in Mbanta, his mother's village. Here, while he experiences the bitterness of

exile, Okonkwo has the opportunity to take refuge with the feminine principle represented by the Earth Goddess and learn the supremacy of a
mother's nurturing love. However, Okonkwo's goals never change. He
works hard to amass wealth through the production of yams, and he dreams
of returning to Umuofia and becoming a judicial leader in the clan. While
Okonkwo single-mindedly works away in Mbanta, however, the Europeans
arrive in Igboland; his friend Obierika visits him twice with news of political and social upheaval. Abame, one of the villages in the union of Umuofia,
is razed by the newcomers, and Christianity is beginning to attract the *osu*,
or the outcasts, and the unsuccessful men of the community, including
Okonkwo's son, Nwoye.

The changes which occur while Oknonkwo is in exile in Mbanta reflect the history of colonization in Nigeria. The Igbo people traded with the
Portuguese in the fifteenth and sixteenth centuries, the Dutch in the seventeenth century, and the British in the eighteenth century. In the nineteenth
century, the Igbo began to trade palm oil for European goods; however,
friendly relations with the British crumbled after 1875 as security on the
Niger River declined and pockets of violence erupted. Although Igboland
had functioned as a British trade colony for decades, it was not formally declared a British Protectorate until 1900. In order to "pacify" Eastern Nigeria, the British destroyed much of Igboland and launched extensive military
expeditions in order to amalgamate northern and southern Nigeria in 1914.
Despite resistance, by 1928 Igbo men were forced to pay taxes, and British
colonialism took hold.

During the colonial era, British officials sought to govern hundreds of
decentralized Igbo villages clustered in various political constructs through
a system of indirect rule. Igbo institutions were replaced with a "native
court," a system that was not administered by leaders who had earned titles
within the community, but rather by appointed warrant chiefs, district offi-
cers, court clerks, and messengers who held no traditional status in the village. Corruption was rampant, and the Igbo resisted the destruction of
indigenous political life and the threat of increased taxation. The resistance
culminated in the Women's War of 1929–1930, which forced the British to
restructure Eastern Nigeria to comply more closely with traditional village
organization.

In Part Three of *Things Fall Apart*, Okonkwo returns from exile in
Mbanta to a tense and radically changed Umuofia. At this point in the
novel, a colonial government is taking root; the palm oil trade is transform-
ing the economy; and Christianity is dividing the clan. Tensions escalate at
the annual worship of the Earth Goddess when the zealous Christian convert Enoch unmasks an *egwugwu*, an Igbo masquerader representing an an-

cestral spirit. His apostasy kills the spirit, unmasks the traditional religion, and throws Umuofia into confusion. Other *egwugwu* are enraged and retaliate by razing Enoch's compound and the new Christian church. Okonkwo and other village leaders are subsequently jailed and whipped by order of the district commissioner. After paying a fine, the humiliated Igbo are released from prison.

The members of Umuofia who have remained loyal to traditional life gather to mourn the abominations suffered by the ancient gods, the ancestors, and the entire Igbo community. They decry the new religion which has pitted Igbo against Igbo. When colonial officials arrive to disperse the crowd, Okonkwo blocks them; he then draws his machete and decapitates the court messenger. Okonkwo marshals no support, however, for the divided Igbo community fails to rise in defense of traditional life. The tragic Okonkwo has no recourse. He retreats and hangs himself from a tree.

Okonkwo fails to achieve immortality according to Igbo tradition. Only strangers may touch him now, for he has committed suicide, the ultimate offense against the Earth Goddess. Okonkwo does not even merit a simple burial among his own people. In the final denouement, a perplexed district commissioner orders Obierika and other members of the Igbo community to appear in court with Okonkwo's corpse. In the closing passage of the novel the district commmissioner reflects upon the book he is writing and decides to allot the tragedy of Okonkwo a paragraph in his anthropological study of the Igbo titled "The Pacification of the Primitive Tribes of the Lower Niger."

The changes introduced in Part Three of *Things Fall Apart* reflect the changes introduced by Christianity in Nigeria. As colonial officials altered the fabric of political and social life, Christian missionaries simultaneously offered respite to the disenfranchised among the Igbo and attacked the foundation of traditional Igbo religion. The Anglican Church Missionary Society established a mission in Onitsha in 1857; later the Roman Catholic Holy Ghost Fathers and Society of African Missions set up stations east and west of the Niger. Christianity offered a message of love to those who did not succeed in the Igbo world. The disenfranchised included the anguished mothers of twins, who were forced to abandon their children in the Evil Forest according to Igbo tradition; the *osu*, despised descendants of religious slave cults; and those unsuccessful men who did not earn titles and achieve traditional wealth and status. Although Christianity offered respite to the marginalized, the new faith rent apart the fabric of traditional Igbo life. The missionaries preached the mystery of the Trinity, but could not understand the Igbo concept of a multidimensional God. The Christians reenacted the

Last Supper, but could not accept the ritual performed by the *egwugwu*, masked elders who ritually represent the ancestral spirits of the village. In addition to the religious dogma, the missionaries condemned polygamy and other traditional Igbo customs.

Furthermore, the missionaries offered the Igbo educational opportunities as they introduced Christianity. Because the colonial government subsidized the mission schools, Christianity became a handmaiden of the colonial government as education became an agent of Christianization. The results were doubled-edged: as more and more Igbo people synthesized Christianity with their traditional faith and assimilated aspects of western culture, the traditional way of life fell apart.

Literary Techniques in **Things Fall Apart**

In *Things Fall Apart*, Chinua Achebe addresses the legacy of colonialism as it has shaped Igbo society and individuals. Yet, the author himself is an educated, westernized Igbo reconstructing traditional life and the age of European imperialism. Nevertheless, unlike his hero Okonkwo, the author strives to maintain his balance as he describes the forces of history. Achebe dramatizes the ambiguity of Igbo culture and traditional religion as he expresses the paradoxically oppressive and liberating forces of colonialism and Christianity.

Chinua Achebe writes in English; however, in order to recreate the cultural milieu of the Igbo people, he Africanizes the language of the novel. Specific Igbo words and complicated names are used freely. Profound philosophical concepts such as *chi* and *ogbanje* are explained in the text or glossary and are fundamental to the story. The use of idioms and proverbs, the "palm oil" of conversation, also clarify the conflict, express different points of view, and instruct the characters as well as the reader. For example, many proverbs affirm Okonkwo in his struggle to achieve greatness in spite of his *chi*, while others warn him to balance life's energies. Short stories and talks on values, such as the importance of bridewealth and respect for elders, are also woven into the text and further serve as subtle lessons on aspects of Igbo life and culture.

Overall, the author's language and narrative techniques immortalize the story of Okonkwo and attempt to recreate the complex precolonial Igbo society. Chinua Achebe teaches the westernized world that civilization and culture existed in Africa long before the coming of the Europeans. However, the author simply tells the tale; it is the reader who must reflect upon this turbulent period of history and evaluate the life of Okonkwo.

Points to Ponder
Literary critics have provided varied interpretations of *Things Fall Apart.* The
question of character is one of the crucial issues for discussion raised by the
novel. Is Okonkwo a typical Igbo striving to achieve success in the traditional world? Is he truly off balance and simply unable to stabilize the masculine and feminine forces in his life? Is he a villain, a victim, or a tragic
hero? What is Okonkwo's tragic flaw? Furthermore, why does the author
have Okonkwo commit suicide at the end of the novel? What does the
death of the protagonist signify? Is Chinua Achebe posing a question about
fate and destiny? Does the personal god-force or *chi* control Okonkwo's fate
or destiny? Is it impossible for one to overcome fate with hard work and
persistence?

Other issues concern the overarching theme of conflict in the novel.
In what ways are the values of the traditional Igbo society and religion in
conflict with the colonial society and the Christian world view? When
groups face change, how does society encourage those people who adhere
to traditional values without ostracizing those people who wish to experi-
ment with new ideas? How can people keep traditional values alive when
other customs and beliefs seem to invade their world? At the end of the
novel, the district commissioner plans to allot Okonkwo a paragraph in his
book about the Igbo; he has titled his work "The Pacification of the Primitive Tribes of the Lower Niger." How would a successful Igbo living in
Umuofia at the time of Okonkwo's death title the commissioner's book?
How would an *osu* or an anguished mother of twins title the commissioner's work?

The portrayal of women in the novel and the concept of cosmic
feminine energy are important discussion points. How are the women
characters presented in the novel, and how does this portrayal of women
contrast with the profound feminine energy of the Earth Goddess? Does
Ani's energy ultimately destroy Okonkwo's life? Or is Okonkwo destroyed by himself or the forces of history? Is he a microcosm of the
larger socially cohesive and religiously oriented Igbo world which col-
lapses from within as it is pounded by the external forces of colonialism
and Christianity?

Finally, what is the significance of the title of the novel, which is ironically drawn from W. B. Yeats' "The Second Coming?" In this poem, Yeats
describes history as a succession of cycles and foresees the Christian era giving way to an unknown future introduced by the second coming of Christ.
Achebe applies Yeats' image to Africa where the traditional world of the
nineteenth century gives way to the colonial regime of the twentieth century. As the gyre of history in which the Igbo civilization turns expands, the

religion and moral code at its center give way to Christianity for, in Yeats' words:

> Turning and turning in the widening gyre
> The falcon cannot hear the falconer;
> Things fall apart; the center cannot hold;
> Mere anarchy is loosed upon the world. . . .

Although the traditional religion orders and civilizes the precolonial world, Christianity takes root in the Evil Forest outside of Umuofia, the dark spot where twins are thrown away and victims like Ikemefuna are sacrificed. Why is Igbo society vulnerable to the promises of Christianity? Does the rigid Igbo code, which both nurtures and negates life, ultimately fail to bend and respect life? Okonkwo never seems to find his balance and takes his own life. Is his inflexibility a tragic flaw which is reflected in the rigidity of Igbo society?

Another discussion may focus on the concept of status. Is power and leadership in traditional Igbo society based on investment in material wealth, titles, and community service? How does status translate into judicial power, and what is the successful Igbo's responsibility to the community? Finally, how does the concept of status in Igbo society compare with the concept of status in modern western society? A more in-depth understanding of traditional Igbo titles is helpful in understanding Okonkwo's motivation and addressing these issues.

Traditional Igbo Titles

Okonkwo reflects traditional Igbo culture which defined success as individual achievement rooted in communal cooperation and group solidarity. Historically, many Igbo villages were simple democracies based upon egalitarian principles ensuring all citizens equal opportunity to achieve success. Success was generally understood as the accumulation of material wealth through hard work. As a title was purchased, wealth was redistributed through the society and benefited not only the individual but also the community. The title-taking system was open to both men and women; however, due to financial responsibilities to children, women did not purchase titles as often as men. Talented men in particular were expected to convert their wealth to titles; this achievement proclaimed prestige and power and allowed greater participation in political and religious life. Titles were generally taken in ascending order, and as the prestige of the title increased, so did its fee. The titles an individual acquired not only measured success and indicated status in Igbo society but actually provided a work role, an identity, and a self-concept for the individual.

The model Igbo attempted to acquire wealth in a dynamic and highly competitive world—an everyday world that was rooted in the divine. An energetic and innovative individual could manipulate some rules in order to achieve a goal; however, some laws, such as those which prohibited abominations against the Earth, could never be compromised. Each individual was also free to work toward a goal in spite of his *chi*, and a successful individual was expected to be alert and adapt quickly to a constantly changing world which offered various work opportunities.

Acquiring a title in Igbo society was not simply a matter of purchasing political power. A title required a general consensus of the community, which was ruled by elders in association with title holders and age grades. A title guaranteed a man's character by certifying that he qualified for the title and in some cases required arduous responsibilities such as providing educational opportunities for the youth and performing community service. The title also provided a normative frame which prescribed behavior for the initiate. Furthermore, an individual who joined a title society made a monetary investment in his future, for as his heavy initiation fee was shared equally among members of the title society, so would he share in the fees of future status seekers. For example, men holding the titles of *obi* and *ndi eze* were among the wealthiest and most politically active members in some Igbo communities. Furthermore, by purchasing the highest titles, a leader was admitted into the community of rulers or *otu ochichi* and initiated into the cults of ancestors or *otu ndichie*. Title societies, like councils of elders, work associations, age-groups, women's associations, secret societies, and religious fraternities cut across village and village group boundaries and provided a cohesiveness to Igbo society. The title system also institutionalized natural leadership ability and developed a political consciousness that opposed a strong centralized authority.

In addition to ensuring power and prestige in life, status seeking was integrated into the spiritual cycle of life, growth, death, and rebirth in the Igbo world view. Men without substantial titles were considered nameless, faceless children or weak women and were buried without honors. On the other hand, great men who achieved the highest title underwent a ritual death and resurrection. By earning the exalted name *ndi ichie*, an Igbo achieved immortality while still on earth. The title system therefore formed an integral part of the Igbo people's social, political, and spiritual life by allowing an individual to work creatively and constructively in order to achieve personal status while benefiting the entire community.

The Author and His Work

Chinua Achebe

Born in 1930, Chinua Achebe spent his early childhood in Ogidi, Nigeria, a large Igbo village located near the famous marketplace of Onitsha. In many ways, he was a child of both the traditional Igbo world and the colonial Christian world. Although members of his extended family practiced the traditional Igbo religion, he was a Christian, for his father, Isaiah Achebe, worked as a catechist for the Church Missionary Society. Although he spoke Igbo at home, he studied in Igbo and English in the mission schools, and at the age of fourteen advanced to the prestigious secondary school known as Government College in Umuahia.

In 1948, Achebe was awarded a scholarship to study medicine at the University College in Ibadan; however, he soon refocused his program on literature, religion, and history. In his exploration of English literature, Achebe was repelled by the fundamental racism of colonial classics such as Joseph Conrad's *Heart of Darkness* and Joyce Cary's *Mister Johnson*. These novels depicted a savage Africa which was humanized only by European colonialism. In reaction to this literature, Achebe expanded his own understanding of the Igbo world with a study of oral accounts and written colonial records; he also published his first essays, editorials, and short stories as the student editor of the *University Herald*.

After graduation, Achebe taught for a brief period. In 1954, he took a position as a broadcaster with the Lagos-based Nigerian Broadcasting Corporation, and from 1961–1966, he served as the director of external broadcasting. It was an important period, for as the country moved toward independence, Achebe's programs helped shape a national identity. During this time, Achebe also wrote his first four novels and became the founding editor of Heinemann's African Writers Series. *Things Fall Apart* was published in 1958, followed by *No Longer at Ease* in 1960, *Arrow of God* in 1964, and *A Man of the People* in 1966.

In 1967 Achebe supported Biafra's secession from Nigeria and left his public broadcasting position in Lagos to become a senior research fellow at the University of Nigeria in Nsukka. He initiated a speaking tour on behalf of Biafra in 1969 and throughout the civil war wrote poetry, short stories, and essays. His poetry was published as *Beware Soul Brother and Other Poems* in 1971 and his stories as *Girls at War and Other Stories* in 1972. His essays were collected and published in *Morning Yet on Creation Day* (1975); *The Trouble with Nigeria* (1983); and *Hopes and Impediments: Selected Essays, 1965–1987* (1988). During this time Achebe also co-edited *Don't Let Him Die: An Anthology of Memorial Poems for Christoper Okigbo* with Dubem Okafor, which was published in 1978, and founded *Okike: An African Journal of New Writing*, which offered a forum for new African writers.

In addition, Chinua Achebe has written several children's books including *Chike and the River* (1966), *The Drum* (1977), and *The Flute* (1977). He has also co-edited two major anthologies with C. L. Innes titled *African Short Stories* (1985) and *The Heinemann Book of Contemporary African Short Stories* (1992). Achebe published his fifth novel, *Anthills of the Savannah*, in 1987.

In addition to his research and writing, over the past twenty years Chinua Achebe has worked for the University of Nigeria as a professor of literature, the director of African studies, and a pro-vice-chancellor. He has also served as a distinguished visiting professor of literature at the University of Massachusetts, the University of Connecticut, City College of New York, and Bard College. Achebe has lectured extensively throughout Africa and the United States, received numerous awards, including the Nigerian National Merit Award, and served as a literary leader through his work as the chairperson of the Society of Nigerian Authors.

Chinua Achebe's Work

Synthesizing the roles of writer, sociologist, historian, philosopher, and anthropologist, Chinua Achebe attempts to retell history from an African perspective. His first four novels focus on the story of the Igbo people and Nigeria from the precolonial period through the first military coup in 1966. Achebe's poetry, short stories, essays, and lectures further develop his fundamental themes and define the writer as an artist and teacher. His most recent novel, *Anthills of the Savannah*, depicts a new unidentified African nation struggling to define itself in the modern world.

Arrow of God, published in 1964, is set in colonial Igboland. The time frame is the early 1920s, after the arrival of Europeans in the 1800s depicted in *Things Fall Apart*, and before the emergence of the corrupt, independent Nigeria depicted in *No Longer at Ease* in 1960. Achebe focuses on Ezeulu, an intellectual religious leader, who may have the capability of adapting to a new world, but who is blocked by the religious and political forces of the community he strives to serve. Ezeulu is the chief priest of the god Ulu and is opposed by supporters of Idemili, a rival god. When tensions erupt in the village union touching off an unjust war, British administrators ask Ezeulu to serve as a warrant chief. Realizing he can control neither traditional nor colonial forces, Ezeulu refuses to support either the warring Igbo or the European oppressors. He believes he can act only as an arrow in the bow of his god, Ulu. He therefore steadfastly obeys Ulu, who tells him not to announce the Feast of the New Yam, a custom which signals the beginning of the planting season. Ezeulu is faithful to his god, but his action causes great suffering. In the end, it seems as if Ulu has destroyed his priest, his people, and himself, for ironically, the distraught villagers reject the traditional religion and send their sons to the Christian church with a peace offering of last year's yams. Ultimately, an individual and community are destroyed as the complicated Igbo belief system succumbs to the inevitable force of history.

Originally conceived as the second half of *Things Fall Apart*, *No Longer at Ease* was written as a sequel to the first novel and published in 1960. The novel takes place in the early days of independence, and the protagonist is Obi Okonkwo, the tragic Okonkwo's grandson. The historical forces that destroyed the elder Okonkwo continue to wreck havoc, for neither the idealist Obi nor the society at large is able to create a just and moral Nigeria. Like his grandfather, Obi walks a delicate line. As a young, idealistic civil servant, he strives to build a new nation devoid of corruption. However, he must respond to financial pressures requiring him to repay the Umuofia Progressive Union for financing his education overseas, contribute to his brothers' education, and maintain a standard of living appropriate to European rank. Initially, Obi succeeds. However, the pressures of traditional and modern life become unbearable as his parents forbid his marriage to his pregnant lover Clara because she is an *osu*, a descendant of a religious slave-cult. When she aborts the child and abandons Obi, the moral center of his life fails to hold. He loses his balance and falls into the bribery and corruption encompassing the new nation. Tragically, as he attempts to regain his moral footing, Obi is put on trial and condemned, not for his personal crimes or public corruption, but for being caught red-handed. Obi is the victim of the same historical circumstances which overwhelmed his grandfather. The moral center of the individual, the community, and the nation cannot hold as traditional and modern values clash; things are simply no longer at ease in the nation.

A Man of the People, published in 1966, is set in an anonymous country similar to independent Nigeria, and, unlike Achebe's previous novels, narrates events contemporaneous with its writing. The story depicts the advanced breakdown of moral life in a blistering and farcical indictment of African leaders. Like Obi Oknonkwo in *No Longer at Ease*, the protagonist, Odili Kamalu, is a university graduate who dreams of building a just, new nation. Although scornful of Chief Nanga, a local politician and a fraudulent member of Parliament, Odili is soon overwhelmed by Nanga's charisma and sucked into the new nation's corrupt system of bribery and nepotism. His public seduction is paralleled by personal humiliation when

Nanga seduces Odili's lover, Elsie. The young politician responds by join-
ing a contending political party and contesting Nanga's seat in Parliament.
Odili fails to unseat his corrupt rival, for a rigged election maintains the
status quo. However, in the final scene, a coup abolishes all political parties, and all the leaders are annihilated, for none of them are true men of
the people. Ironically, these fictional events describe the military coup
staged in Nigeria in January 1966, just before the Biafran crisis. Consequently, the publication of the novel, also in January 1966, attracted con-
siderable attention. This tragically realistic tale about the absurd and
irresponsible behavior of Nigerian politicians completes Achebe's series of
four novels dramatizing the cataclysmic changes that shook the people of
Igboland and Nigeria during a period of time stretching from the 1800s
to the 1960s.

   During the Biafran war and its aftermath, Achebe wrote poetry, short
stories, and a variety of critical essays. *Beware Soul Brother and Other Poems*,
published in 1971, expresses Achebe's anguish over Nigeria's tragic civil
war. His stories, collected as *Girls at War and Other Stories* and published in
1972, highlight a variety of themes revealing the complexities of traditional
and modern life in Africa. Achebe's essays underscore many of his themes,
include literary criticism, and define the writer's role. His major collections
include: *Morning Yet on Creation Day* published in 1975; *The Trouble with
Nigeria* published in 1983; and *Hopes and Impediments: Selected Essays,
1965–1987* published in 1988. In one of his most influential essays, titled
"The Novelist as Teacher," Achebe maintains that the writer must educate
his readers to social and political realities. In a seminal essay titled "The
African Writer and the English Language," he acknowledges that English is
a colonial tool that carries an oppressor's world view; however, he champions the creative manipulation of English to express the African experience.
Achebe believes that African literature written in English is valid and should
stand beside African literature written in indigenous languages such as
Swahili, Kikuyu, Igbo, and Zulu.

   In 1987, Achebe published his long-awaited novel *Anthills of the Savannah*, which fictionalizes many of his political concerns. This novel is set in the
imaginary country of Kangan and focuses on the creation of the modern nation-state in West Africa. A cruel military dictator named Sam has seized control of a civilian government and attempts to starve the dissident Abazon, a
traditional and cohesive ethnic group, into submission. Because he fails to
understand the contribution of a traditional nation in the process of building
a modern nation-state, Sam is killed in another coup. Ikem Osodi is the editor of *The National Gazette* and Kangan's leading poet. He believes that the
modern nation-state must grow from the traditional nations and will include

the proletariat as well as the intellectual elite; however, he is murdered by Sam's repressive regime. Christopher Oriko, Ikem's friend, sits in Sam's cabinet as the commissioner for information and believes that the modern nation-state can be created from the top down. He is open-minded and seeks to understand the traditional culture's desire for self-determination; however, he is killed as he attempts to prevent the rape of a Muslim woman on his journey to the hinterland of Abazon. In the end, feminine energy presides over the birth of the new modern nation-state. The friends of the deceased Ikem and Christopher share a common communion rite as they break the kola nut, remember the dead, and celebrate the birth of a newborn child. This baby girl is the offspring of Ikem, the intellectual, and his girlfriend Elewa, the market woman. Beatrice, Christopher's fiancée, names the child Amaechina, a masculine name that means "may the path never close." It is a gathering of friends, not strangers, who mourn death and celebrate life. Like the anthills in the savannah that survive to tell the newborn grass about last year's scorching sun and blistering brush fires, the memories of Chris and Ikem stand as warnings to the newborn nation-state. They remind the young that a strong independent nation-state must grow out of traditional nations, must peacefully combine ethnic groups, and must include the proletariat as well as the intellectual elite.

As a critic and teacher, Chinua Achebe defines the writer's responsibilities to his art and society. His themes seek to express the wisdom, the tragedy, and the truth about Africa. The author invites the reader to react to the plight of societies profoundly affected by colonialism and judge the moral dilemma of individual characters. The use of Igbo words, local dialects, proverbs, anecdotes, and traditional tales season and spice his plots, authenticate his heroes' stories, and attempt to recreate a dynamic African world.

Resources

DAVIES, CAROLE BOYCE. "Motherhood in the Works of Male and Female Igbo Writers: Achebe, Emecheta, Nwapa, and Nzekwu." In *Ngambika: Studies of Women in African Literature*, 241–256. Trenton, N.J.: African World Press, 1986. Discussion of Achebe's female principle and comparative analysis of the concept of motherhood.

DUERDEN, DENNIS, ed. "Chinua Achebe." In *African Writers Talking*, 2–17. New York: Africana Publishing Company, 1972. Excerpts of interviews with Chinua Achebe conducted between 1962–1967.

GIKANDI, SIMON. *Reading Chinua Achebe: Language and Ideology in Fiction.* London: Heinemann, 1991. An analysis of construction of "nation" in Achebe's novels.

———. "Chinua Achebe and the Invention of African Literature." Introduction to Chinua Achebe's *Things Fall Apart*, ix–xvii. Portsmouth, N.H.: Heinemann, 1996.

GUNNER, ELIZABETH. "*Things Fall Apart* and *No Longer at Ease*." In *A Handbook for Teaching African Literature*, 45–55. London: Heinemann, 1984. Two brief units with interesting discussion questions and reading links for students.

HARROW, KENNETH. "Flying Without Perching—Metaphor, Proverb, and Gendered Discourse." In *Thresholds of Change in African Literature: The Emergence of a Tradition,* 109–137. Portsmouth, N.H.: Heinemann, 1994. An insightful discussion of Achebe's use of the proverb and the overarching theme in *Things Fall Apart.*

INNES, C. L. *Chinua Achebe.* New York: Cambridge University Press, 1990. A comprehensive examination of Achebe's life and work in the context of Nigerian culture and politics.

INNES, C. L., and BERNTH LINDFORS. *Critical Perspectives on Chinua Achebe.* Portsmouth, N.H.: Heinemann, 1979. A collection of critical essays on the basic themes and narrative techniques of *Things Fall Apart, No Longer at Ease, Arrow of God,* and *A Man of the People.*

IRELE, ABIOLA. "The Tragic Conflict in the Novels of Chinua Achebe." In C. L. Innes, ed., *Critical Perspectives on Chinua Achebe,* 10–21. Portsmouth, N.H.: Heinemann, 1979. A review of the basic themes and conflicts in Achebe's first four novels.

ISICHEI, ELIZABETH. *A History of the Igbo People.* New York: St. Martin's Press, 1976. A basic history of Igboland from prehistoric times through the colonial period and its aftermath.

IYASERE, SOLOMON O. "Narrative Techniques in *Things Fall Apart.*" In C. L. Innes, ed., *Critical Perspectives on Chinua Achebe,* 92–110. Portsmouth, N.H.: Heinemann, 1979. An analysis of techniques such as proverbs, folk tales, rituals, and episodes which weave complex themes such as individualism, community solidarity, and colonialism together in *Things Fall Apart.*

KILLAM, G. D. *The Novels of Chinua Achebe.* New York: Africana Publishing Company, 1969. A basic overview of the structures, central themes, and characters in *Things Fall Apart, No Longer at Ease, Arrow of God,* and *A Man of the People,* with an analysis of Okonkwo as an archetype of Igbo culture.

KORTENAAR, NEIL TEN. "Only Connect: *Anthills of the Savannah* and Achebe's *Trouble with Nigeria.*" In *Research in African Literatures* 24, 3 (Fall 1993): 59–72. A discussion of nation and the vision of the inter-ethnic modern nation-state presented in *Anthills of the Savannah.*

LINDFORS, BERNTH. "The Palm-Oil with Which Achebe's Words Are Eaten." In C. L. Innes, ed., *Critical Perspectives on Chinua Achebe,* 47–66. Portsmouth, N.H.: Heinemann, 1979. An analysis of Achebe's use of proverbs and similes.

———, ed. *Approaches to Teaching Things Fall Apart.* New York: Modern Language Association of America, 1991. Various suggestions for teaching the novel.

MOYERS, BILL. "Chinua Achebe: Nigerian Novelist." In B. S. Flowers, ed., *A World of Ideas,* 333–344. New York: Doubleday, 1989. The transcript of an interview with Achebe aired on Public Broadcasting Service shortly after the publication of *Anthills of the Savannah.*

———. "Chinua Achebe: Nigerian Novelist." PBS Video, 1320 Braddock Place, Alexandria, VA 22314. Phone: 800-424-7963. Videotape of the Public Broadcasting Service interview with Achebe.

MUONEKE, ROMANUS OKEY. *Art, Rebellion, and Redemption: A Reading of the Novels of Chinua Achebe.* New York: Peter Lang, 1994. An analysis of the relationship between the writer and society with a discussion of rebellion in Nigeria and the theme of redemption in Achebe's novels.

OBIECHINA, EMMANUEL. "Narrative Proverbs in the African Novel." In *Research in African Literatures* 24, 4 (Winter 1993): 123–140. An analysis of the narrative techniques in *Things Fall Apart.*

OGBAA, KALU. *Gods, Oracles, and Divination: Folkways in Chinua Achebe's Novels.* Trenton, N.J.: Africa World Press, 1992. A discussion of Achebe's presentation of traditional Igbo religion, customs, and folk language with sections on names, proverbs, stories, and songs.

OHADIKE, DON C. *Anioma: A Social History of the Western Igbo People.* Athens: Ohio University Press, 1994. A history of the Igbo people west of the Niger River with an interesting section on traditional Igbo titles.

———. "Igbo Culture and History." Introduction to Chinua Achebe, *Things Fall Apart*, xix–xlix. Portsmouth, N.H.: Heinemann, 1996. An overview of Igbo history, social organization, culture, and religion.

OKOYE, EMMANUEL MEZIEMADU. *The Traditional Religion and its Encounter with Christianity in Achebe's Novels.* New York: Peter Lang, 1987. A review of Igbo religion as presented by Achebe and ethnographic literature including detailed definitions of traditional religious concepts.

PETERSON, KIRSTEN HOLST, and ANNA RUTHERFORD, eds. *Chinua Achebe: A Celebration.* Portsmouth, N.H.: Heinemann, 1991. A collection of writing celebrating Achebe's contribution to world literature.

PRIEBE, RICHARD. "The Proverb, Realism, and Achebe: A Study of Ethical Consciousness." In *Myth, Realism, and the West African Writer*, 47–55. Trenton, N.J.: Africa World Press, 1988. A discussion of language and the structural parallels between the stories of Oedipus, Job, and Okonkwo.

QUAYSON, ATO. "Realism, Criticism, and the Disguises of Both: A Reading of Chinua Achebe's *Things Fall Apart* with an Evaluation of the Criticism Relating to It." In *Research in African Literatures* 25, 4 (Winter 1994): 115–136. A review of recent criticism on *Things Fall Apart*.

STOCK, A. G. "Yeats and Achebe." In C. L. Innes, ed., *Critical Perspectives on Chinua Achebe*, 86–92. Portsmouth, N.H.: Heinemann, 1979. A discussion of the source, imagery, and symbolism of the title *Things Fall Apart*.

UCHENDU, VICTOR C. *The Igbo of Southeast Nigeria.* New York: Holt, Rinehart and Winston, 1965. A basic anthropological case study of the Igbo people including a discussion of religion, customs, government, and family.

WILKINSON, JANE. "Chinua Achebe." In *Talking with African Writers*, 46–57. Portsmouth, N.H.: Heinemann, 1992. A sensitive interview about the role of the artist vis-à-vis the Nigerian regime with a focus on *Anthills of the Savannah*.

WREN, ROBERT. *Achebe's World: The Historical and Cultural Context of the Novels of Chinua Achebe.* Harlow, England: Longman Studies in African Literature, 1980. Important historical and anthropological background illuminating Achebe's first four novels.

A Selected Bibliography of Chinua Achebe's Work

Things Fall Apart. London: Heinemann, 1958; Portsmouth, N.H.: Heinemann, 1996.

No Longer at Ease. London: Heinemann, 1960; Portsmouth, N.H.: Heinemann, 1987.

Arrow of God. London: Heinemann, 1964; Portsmouth, N.H.: Heinemann, 1988.

Chike and the River. Cambridge: Cambridge University Press, 1966.

A Man of the People. Portsmouth, N.H.: Heinemann, 1966.

Beware Soul Brother and Other Poems. Enugu, Nigeria: Nwankwo–Ifejika, 1971; London: Heinemann, 1972.

Girls at War and Other Stories. Portsmouth, N.H.: Heinemann, 1972.

How the Leopard Got His Claws. With John Iroaganachi. New York: The Third Press, 1973.

Morning Yet on Creation Day: Essays. Portsmouth, N.H.: Heinemann, 1975.

The Drum. Enugu, Nigeria: Fourth Dimension, 1977.

The Flute. Enugu, Nigeria: Fourth Dimension, 1977.

Don't Let Him Die: An Anthology of Memorial Poems for Christopher Okigbo. Edited with Dubem Okafor. Enugu, Nigeria: Fourth Dimension, 1978.

The Trouble with Nigeria. Portsmouth, N.H.: Heinemann, 1983.

African Short Stories. Edited with C. L. Innes. Portsmouth, N.H.: Heinemann, 1985.

Anthills of the Savannah. London: Heinemann, 1987; Portsmouth, N.H.: Heinemann, 1988.

Hopes and Impediments: Selected Essays, 1965–1987. Portsmouth, N.H.: Heinemann, 1988.

The Heinemann Book of Contemporary African Short Stories. Edited with C. L. Innes. Portsmouth, N.H.: Heinemann, 1992.

NIGERIA

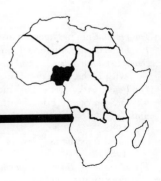

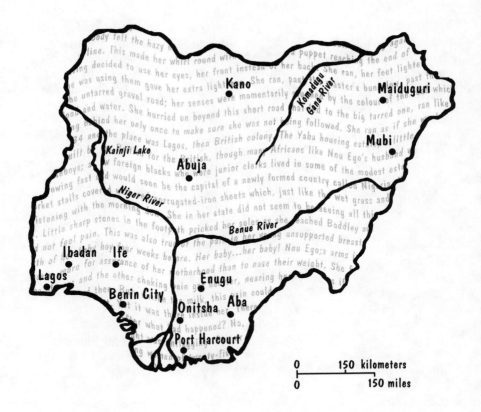

Kano

Maiduguri

Komadugu
Gana River

Mubi

Kainji Lake

Abuja

Niger River

Benue River

Ibadan   Ife

Lagos

Benin City

Enugu

Onitsha   Aba

Port Harcourt

```
0        150 kilometers
|_____|
0        150 miles
```

CHINUA ACHEBE AND BUCHI EMECHETA WRITE ABOUT THE IGBO
PEOPLE OF NIGERIA. IGBO IS ONE OF MORE THAN 250 LANGUAGES
SPOKEN IN MODERN NIGERIA.

Chapter 2

Buchi Emecheta and
The Joys of Motherhood

Buchi Emecheta is one of West Africa's most prolific women writers. In novels translated into over fourteen languages, she addresses the role of African women in history and society. Her perspective in *The Joys of Motherhood* is profound and complex, for she shatters the flat, one-sided images of African women depicted as obedient daughters, silent companions, submissive wives, long-suffering mothers, mindless clerks, stupid secretaries, and frivolous good-time girls. Published in 1979, the novel raises the issues of a woman's identity and role in society. Nnu Ego, the protagonist, is an Igbo woman constrained by traditional society, the colonial world, her marriages, motherhood, and above all by her own concept of womanhood. Nnu Ego loses her sense of self and sacrifices her life for her children. It is questionable whether she truly experiences any true joy in motherhood.

The Joys of Motherhood and the Igbo Women of Nigeria
The Joys of Motherhood is suitable for students on the lower or intermediate levels in literature courses and women's studies programs. The novel focuses on the life of an Igbo woman whose concept of self is inextricably bound by her concept of motherhood. Nnu Ego is consumed by her desire and responsibility to conceive, deliver, nurture, and educate children. Nnu Ego is introduced in a flashback as suicidal after the death of her first son. Then, her story is told in two parts: initially, the life and death of her proud mother Ona and her first marriage to the handsome Amatokwu; and finally, her second marriage to the Lagos laundryman Nnaife.

The first section of the novel reveals Nnu Ego's family history. Her mother, Ona, was a beauty who chose to remain in her father's household. Although she was extremely independent, Ona sustained a turbulent relationship with her arrogant lover, Chief Agbadi, who disdained his own wives as they sank into domestic responsibilities and motherhood. Chief Agbadi remained fascinated by the heartless Ona who refused to marry him, and conquered her sexually in the courtyard of his compound. Nnu

Ego was born from this union. Oddly, however, Nnu Ego's mother, Ona, chose not to marry the great Chief Agbadi, but rather to produce children who would be raised in her father's homestead.

Shortly after Agbadi's sexual conquest of Ona, his senior wife, Agunwa, became ill and died. Although she had suffered shame and public humiliation, Agunwa was lauded as a complete woman and a quiet mother of sons. She was buried with her personal slave, a beautiful young woman who begged for her life. Before she was slashed in the head with a cutlass and forced back into the grave with her mistress, the beautiful slave woman promised to return to Agbadi's household as a legitimate daughter. It is the spirit of this slave woman who becomes Nnu Ego's *chi*, or the personal god-force that will guide her through life. However, before Ona herself died, she begged Agbadi to allow Nnu Ego to have a life of her own—to be a woman unfettered by society and encouraged to marry only if she desired.

In the third chapter of the novel, Nnu Ego marries a strong, handsome young man named Amatokwu in a neighboring village. However, she is soon rejected by her husband because she is unable to conceive. Her inability to mother children makes her feel like an incomplete and undesirable person. When the dissatisfied Amatokwu takes a second wife who immediately conceives and bears a son, Nnu Ego is no longer treated as a senior wife but rather as hired farm labor. Amatokwu refuses to waste his precious seed on the infertile Nnu Ego any longer and allows her to return to her father's compound. Because of her failure to conceive with Amatokwu, Nnu Ego is discarded, shamed by the husband she loves, and ostracized by society. In her first marriage, Nnu Ego fails to fulfill her mother's wish, for she has not only allowed herself to be constrained by marriage and society, but she herself believes that her only value as a person and as a woman lies in her ability to mother children.

The first section of the novel takes place in traditional Igbo villages. In many ways, Nnu Ego reflects the women of the traditional Igbo world who were expected to marry and produce many children. After marriage, a woman's status was enhanced by motherhood, and virtually all traditional marriages were polygamous in order to ensure many children to cultivate crops. In fact, a man with only one wife was considered poor and therefore denied the right to purchase the highly esteemed title of *eze*.

Furthermore, a woman who increased her husband's lineage was also respected because children were considered a reincarnation of the ancestors and protection against poverty in old age. Although the Igbo understood the reproductive process, conception was complicated by the belief that deities, deceased ancestors, and other spirits must be willing to reincarnate themselves before a woman could conceive. Birth was also connected with the spirit world, for every child was born with a *chi* or personal god-force.

Irregularities in giving birth were also understood in spiritual terms. The continual birth of offspring who died during childhood was understood as the cycle of an *ogbanje*, or a child who is born, dies, and continually reenters its mother's womb to be reborn and die again. Traditionally the Igbo also believed that multiple births degraded humans to the level of animals. Therefore, the birth of twins was tragic, for the mother was isolated and the infants abandoned in the forest. Regardless of these complexities, however, in the traditional Igbo world, womanhood was largely defined as motherhood.

Nevertheless, traditional society did offer other opportunities for women, including farming, fishing, herding, commerce, and industrial labor such as the production of pottery, the design and manufacture of cloth and clothing, and the creation of crafts. In many communities, women had the right to keep the proceeds of their labor and were then free to translate their wealth into prestigious titles and political power. For example, rural women augmented the yam crop produced by men with melon, okra, maize, pumpkins, beans, cocoyams, and cassava. In the early twentieth century, cassava became the staple food in some areas, allowing the "cassava women" to improve their own social and economic status in society. Cassava production also allowed women to control the running of local markets, which served not only as loci of trade, but also as important village centers of socialization where ceremonies, title taking, business transactions, and meetings took place. As a result, many women farmers became independent and wielded real economic power.

Some successful women traders and farmers also transferred their wealth into association memberships and titles; most, however, chose to plow their finances into the well-being and education of their children or supplied cash for their poor husbands to purchase titles. The women of Anioma in western Nigeria illustrate the power of the women's economic and political associations. Here any woman who could finance her initiation ceremonies was admitted to the *otu omu* society. This women's council controlled the local marketplace by imposing fines on anyone who disturbed the peace and punishing anyone who violated the social taboos of incest and adultery. The highest title in the association was the *omu* or queen of the society, which was an elected position. The *omu* and other society leaders sat at the general councils of chiefs and elders where they participated in various aspects of community leadership and decision making.

Other village associations in Anioma included the *otu umu ada*, or the association of women born to a lineage in a specific town, and the *otu inyeme di*, or the association of women married to men of a lineage in a specific town. These groups allowed women to influence the politics and social life in their hometowns and the towns in which they lived as wives and mothers. For example, if the village or marketplace rules were ignored, an association could easily organize strikes and boycotts, "make war" (cause a disturbance), or "sit on a man" (exert pressure on someone who was unjust). Overall, the women's associations acted as political pressure groups and provided a system of checks and balances ensuring the equity of both men and women in traditional society.

In the second section of *The Joys of Motherhood*, Nnu Ego moves to colonial Lagos to marry the laundryman Nnaife Owulum. Arriving on his doorstep sight-unseen, Nnu Ego is repulsed by her ugly new husband who himself acts as a slave washing the colonial masters' clothing. She cringes as he handles the white woman's bras and panties and tolerates Nnaife only in the hopes of becoming a mother. When she finally does conceive, she gradually begins to function as an adult in the society by starting her own business with capital borrowed from the Ibuza women's fund. Her joy is short-lived, however, for four weeks after the birth of her first son, Ngozi, the child is dead. Nnu Ego believes she has once again failed as a woman. Her only recourse is suicide.

But Nnu Ego is rescued and given another chance at life. She conceives a second time and through a dream, her *chi* reveals that she may have as many hungry, dirty babies as she wishes. Her newborn son is named Oshia, and Nnu Ego vows to discontinue her trading and depend on Nnaife's earnings in order to devote herself solely to motherhood. However, Nnaife not only faces unemployment, but he also soon becomes the head of his extended family when he inherits his brother's five wives and countless children. The stunned Nnu becomes a senior wife and continues to validate her womanhood by giving birth to three more children: a second son named Adim and twin daughters named Taiwo and Kehinde. As Nnaife fails to provide money for food and household expenses, Nnu Ego finds herself responsible for the welfare of her family.

Pregnant again, Nnu Ego struggles to develop a business by trading cigarettes and other petty items as Nnaife is drafted into the Nigerian forces fighting in Burma during World War II. Her third son is born soon after her father, Agbadi, dies, and Nnu Ego names him Nnamdio, which means "this is my father." Nnu Ego continues to perform her duties in Lagos as a kind of "female husband," because she functions as the head of the household and supervisor of her children and her husband's younger wife while Nnaife is away. She uses the money she earns and the salary Nnaife sends her to feed and educate her children, especially her sons. Upon her husband's return, however, she conceives again, and he ironically provides household help for her in the form of his new, sixteen-year-old wife who is also pregnant.

As Nnu Ego's sense of duty weighs like a chain of slavery around her neck, she sacrifices her life for her children and remains a prisoner of her own flesh and blood. She gives birth to a second set of twin daughters named Obiageli and Malachi, and soon becomes pregnant again. This time the exhausted Nnu Ego gives birth to a stillborn baby and blames herself for the lifeless child.

In spite of her hardships, Nnu Ego is lauded as the mother of very clever children. Oshia wins a scholarship to the United States and continues to squeeze his parents financially dry; Adim also goes on to school and travels to Canada. The quiet Taiwo marries a young, well-educated clerk, and Kehinde ventures across ethnic lines by choosing a Yoruba husband. Nnaife condemns Kehinde and assaults her lover. His actions land him in court where Nnu Ego defends him as the head of the family even though she basically raised her children single-handedly. Nnaife is imprisoned but soon released—a man broken by the pressures of raising a family in a world of changing values.

As Nnu Ego returns to her father's village at the end of the novel, she regrets she did not cultivate deeper friendships with other women and questions her entire life's work. Nnu Ego lived her life believing that children made a woman, a traditional value she learned in her father's compound, yet certainly not a value held by her proud mother Ona. Alone—without a husband, a friend, or a child to comfort her—Nnu Ego simply lays down by the side of the road and dies.

Nnu Ego died before her seven children could give her a good life. When her eldest son Oshia finally returns, he displays his own status by giving his mother a lavish second burial and constructing a shrine in her name. However, Nnu Ego never answers the prayers of infertile women who implore her help and beg for children. Indeed, Nnu Ego leaves the reader wondering about the joys of motherhood.

In the second section of the novel, Nnu Ego reflects the Igbo women who worked together to maintain control over local markets in cities during the colonial era. Women dominated the marketplace through speculative retail trade in palm liquor, sugar, cigarettes, matches, soap, and kola nuts. Some women retailed fish and cakes purchased from local women petty-traders while others held the monopoly over hot cooked food in the marketplace. However, like Nnu Ego's business, the scale of most retail operations remained extremely small due to the lack of capital and spendable income. For example, matches were often sold in half-penny unit boxes, and cigarettes were sold individually. Soap was distributed in single bars or penny envelope packets; writing pads were divided into four-sheet penny units, and even kerosene was sold in penny amounts.

Many women, however, demonstrated much greater political power in confronting and rejecting colonial oppression than Nnu Ego. For example, in 1925 a band of women appeared before a corrupt warrant chief's house

Does Nnu Ego truly experience the joys of motherhood?

in Okigwi and delivered a political message through song and dance. They demanded social reforms such as fixed market prices, boycotted corrupt native courts, and called for extended rights in traditional customs—in particular, a limitation on bride price and integrity in marriage negotiations. When the colonial administration threatened to tax women as well as men in 1928, thousands of Igbo women organized to "make war" or "sit on" the colonial administration. They punished tax collectors and other corrupt officials, burned buildings, destroyed jails, released prisoners, attacked the native courts, and looted European stores. More than fifty women were killed and many more injured. The uprising, known as the Women's War of 1928–1930, forced the colonial administration to reexamine its policies and investigate the injustices suffered by women. As a result, the British attempted to restore precolonial political systems by reinstating the authority of lineage heads and recreating village councils. The native courts system was revised, and half of all taxes collected were allocated for local projects.

The Igbo women of colonial Nigeria expressed their profound desire to return to a just, traditional society and demonstrated their ability to cooperate and achieve a common goal. Although the Igbo people were unable to reconstruct the traditional system of government, Igbo women made an outstanding contribution to political and social reform and shaped the history of Nigeria.

Literary Techniques in The Joys of Motherhood

Buchi Emecheta approaches Nnu Ego as an individual and explores women's experience vis-à-vis men in a male-dominated society in *The Joys of Motherhood.* The author combines her insight into the female psyche with her understanding of painful personal dilemmas and the conflict of traditional and modern values. Although Emecheta denies she is a feminist, her work is dedicated to women and reveals a sensitive and profound understanding of women's experience.

Emecheta begins her novel *in medias res.* The first chapter opens in Lagos in 1934 as Nnu Ego discovers she has miscarried her first child and attempts suicide. A flashback in the second chapter propels the reader to the distant Igbo village of Ogboli. Here the author recounts the story of Nnu Ego's proud mother, Ona, and the beautiful slave woman; these stories provide both a foil and a blueprint for Nnu Ego's life. Chapter Three recounts Nnu Ego's early life in the compound of her first husband, Amatokwu. This segment likewise sets the stage for Nnu Ego's second marriage. The remainder of the novel picks up the story of Nnu Ego from the initial flashback and describes her quest for motherhood.

Buchi Emecheta uses irony as a literary technique to set the mood and develop the theme and characters in the novel. The author analyzes the ironic fate of women in African society and asks the protagonist to re-examine her suffering and determine whether or not she is author of her own misfortune. Suspense propels the plot, and humor combines with vivid imagery in describing characters such as Nnaife, the laundryman with the belly like a pregnant cow and puffy cheeks that appear stuffed with hot yams.

Points to Ponder

The question of Nnu Ego's character is one of the crucial issues for discussion raised by the novel. Is Nnu Ego, the daughter of the powerful chief Agbadi and the proud beauty Ona, independent in spirit like her mother? How does Ona stand as a foil to Nnu Ego? On the other hand, is Nnu Ego actually the reincarnation of the unfortunate slave woman buried alive soon after she was conceived? Has Nnu Ego been guided by the *chi*, or personal god-force, of this slave woman, and has she in fact lived a life of slavery focusing her entire life on her children? In what ways has her life as the mother of so many children been a life of slavery? Moreover, Nnu Ego leaves one unhappy marriage for another; is she therefore responsible for her own unhappiness? What traditional values does Nnu Ego choose to maintain?

The conflict within the story of Nnu Ego is underscored by the history of the Igbo women. Although motherhood was extremely important in the traditional world, Igbo women enjoyed economic and political opportunities and were not limited to the roles of wife and mother. In addition to the constraints of her *chi*, Nnu Ego is also constrained by traditional society and the colonial world of Lagos. How is Nnu Ego in conflict with traditional society, colonial society, her husbands, her children, and herself? What is the fundamental cause of Nnu Ego's unhappiness? Does the colonial world present Nnu Ego with more opportunities than the traditional world offered? Does Nnu Ego take advantage of the opportunities offered by both the traditional and colonial worlds? What is the relationship of motherhood to womanhood? Must a woman become a mother in order to be a complete person?

The comparative analysis of women in the novel is also important. How are the various women portrayed? What is the stance of the more determined and vocal women such as Ona and the slave woman of Agbadi's senior wife, Agunwa? Why does Ona refuse to marry Agbadi? Does the slave woman become a legitimate member of Agbadi's family by becoming Nnu Ego's enslaving *chi*? Other woman such as Agunwa are silent, obedient wives and mothers; how does Nnu Ego reflect this silence as she raises her own children? Is Nnu Ego's silence at the end of the novel her greatest statement? How does Nnu Ego's daughter Kehinde compare with the other women in the novel? Why is she so bold?

In many ways, Buchi Emecheta's *The Joys of Motherhood* reflects the myth of womanhood passed down by generations of mothers. The title of the novel echoes the sad tale told by Flora Nwapa entitled *Efuru*. Efuru is a beautiful, talented, and generous woman who has been chosen to worship the river goddess and therefore must remain unmarried and childless. Emecheta's title, *The Joys of Motherhood*, connects with the final lines of Nwapa's novel as Efuru dreams of the woman of the lake who "had lived for ages at the bottom of the lake. She was as old as the lake itself. She was happy, she was wealthy. She was beautiful. She gave women beauty and wealth but she had no child. She had never experienced the joy of motherhood. Why then did the women worship her?" (*Efuru*, p. 221) How does Nnu Ego connect with the women at the bottom of the lake? What is the meaning of the title of Emecheta's novel? Does Nnu Ego experience any joy in motherhood or has she completely sacrificed her life for the lives of her children? Does her refusal to answer the prayers of infertile women after her death confirm her as a tragic heroine destroyed by society, her family, and her own perception of herself? Or does the author begin to paint a portrait of a new African woman through Nnu Ego's silence?

Another discussion may focus on why Nnu Ego did not choose to become a "male daughter" and heir to her father's property, and how Nnu Ego is a type of "female husband." In both cases, women assumed male responsibilities and enjoyed male privileges by becoming the heads of households. Nnu Ego certainly takes on the role of the head of the household in Lagos; does she enjoy any privileges connected with this role? A more in-depth study of the flexibility of gender roles within traditional society may be helpful in understanding these concepts.

Gender in Traditional Igbo Society

Although customs differed throughout Igbo territory, historically, the concept of gender in traditional society was flexible and separate from the concept of biological sex. Females like Ona and Nnu Ego could take on male gender roles in two basic ways: they could become male daughters and heirs to their fathers' property, or they could become female husbands to other women. In both cases, women assumed male responsibilities and enjoyed male privileges by becoming the heads of households.

Among many Igbo groups, property included land as well as the control of human labor, in particular, women's productive and reproductive power. For example, in the village of Nnobi, land was the major economic resource and generally inherited by male heirs. However, because land was scarce, the society instituted the concept of male daughters, which allowed women to remain in their fathers' homes. These women retained their biological female nature but took on the status of sons by inheriting their fathers' property. The practice was called *nhayikwa* or *nhanye*, a kind of replacement of female status with male status.

Another custom instituted by the Nnobi society was known as woman-to-woman marriage, or *igba ohu*, which allowed women to become female husbands and gain access to land and wealth. The prestigious *Ekwe* title was associated with the goddess Idemili and taken by industrious women with economic potential and leadership ability. This title allowed a woman to pay a bride price in order to marry another woman. The female husband claimed her wife's services and labor, requiring her to trade, farm, tend livestock, or engage in other money-making endeavors. Often the wife would take a lover or another designated male companion in order to bear children in the name of her female husband. The great *Ekwe* women often had male husbands and children of their own yet married many wives, thereby creating and controlling tremendous human resources and wealth. As wives worked for their female husband, they retained the status and customary rights of a wife. Likewise, the female husband retained the customary rights of a man over his wife.

In sum, both male daughters and female husbands were known as *di-bu-no*, a genderless term which indicated one's position as head of his or her family. Ironically, as traditional society became subject to British colonialism, many women married to polygamous male husbands often worked hard to support and educate their children without the financial support of their spouse. In some ways these hardworking women were like single traditional female husbands, or women who acted as heads of households.

The Author and Her Work

Buchi Emecheta

Buchi Emecheta was born in Lagos in 1944, and lost her father, a railway porter, when she was very young. Nevertheless, at the age of ten, she won a scholarship to the Methodist Girls High School in Lagos where she learned English and aspired to become a writer. She punctuated her school days with visits to Ibuza, her family's village, where she listened to tales spun by expert storytellers. Her mother, a six-foot-tall woman nicknamed "Blakie the Black," regarded her daughter as moody and mysterious; she died before Emecheta was seventeen. Feeling society's pressure, at the age of sixteen Emecheta married Sylvester Onwordi, a handsome young man who aspired to study in England. She secured a good job at the American Embassy in Lagos, and by the time she was eighteen, had given birth to two children, Chiedu and Ik.

Emecheta and her husband then emigrated to England, where she worked at the North Finchley Library and soon gave birth to two more children, Jake and Christy. Her husband, who proved to be an eternal student, refused to work and amused himself with other women. During these trying days, Emecheta wrote her first novel titled *The Bride Price*. Sylvester burned her only copy of the manuscript and with it, her dream of being an ideal wife and mother went up in smoke. She took a position in the British Museum, collected her four children, and left her husband. However, Sylvester soon stalked her and raped her; Emecheta consequently conceived, and gave birth to her fifth child, Alice.

As a single mother of five young children, Buchi Emecheta secured a grant to study sociology in London. She quickly related sociological theories and principles to the reality of her own life and began to write. She labored tirelessly to persuade publishers to read her work, and finally her articles were published as a column entitled "Life in the Ditch" in the *New Statesman*. Doors were suddenly opened, and her first, semi-autobiographical novel entitled *In the Ditch* appeared in 1972 when she was an undergraduate student.

Today, Buchi Emecheta lives and writes in England and travels widely. She has taught briefly at the University of Calabar in Nigeria and has been an inspiration to countless young writers. One of her sons is an aspiring author, and her daughter Christy edited her autobiography, *Head Above Water*, published in 1986.

Buchi Emecheta's Work

Emecheta is a prolific writer who delves into the recesses of her own life, the history of her ancestors, and the souls of African women in various social strata and cultures. She maintains an equilibrium between the sociologist's objectivity and the artist's passion by offering her readers insight into women as real people who struggle with the paradoxes of life. Her work crisscrosses cultural barriers and introduces aspects of African life to the western reader.

Buchi Emecheta's semi-autobiographical novel *In the Ditch*, published in 1972, recounts aspects of the author's failed marriage and life as an expatriate in London. The protagonist, Adah Obi, who is separated from her husband Francis, struggles to care for her five children, maintain a position at the British Museum, and complete her education. In addition, Adah faces a hostile Nigerian landlord, who exploits her by charging exorbitant rents and resorting to witchcraft in order to drive her out. Adah loathes her corrupt landlord who personifies the expatriate Nigerian community's response to her situation. She finds his "juju," or power, to be incoherent and ineffective but also finds herself alone between two worlds. Struggling to integrate herself into a new culture by adapting her traditional values, Adah realizes that she must resign her museum position in order to care for her children. Because she receives no support from her own people, she turns to the British welfare system. Here she finds comfort in the friendship and generosity of poor English women, who, like herself, are "in the ditch." Although she learns what it means to be poor, black, and female in England, she also learns to cross racial lines and stand in solidarity with other disenfranchised women subsisting in the modern world.

Emecheta continues the semi-autobiographical story of Adah Obi in *Second-Class Citizen*, which was published in 1974. This novel introduces Adah as a child in her uncle's household in Nigeria. Although she has completed secondary school, Adah cannot attend Ibadan University, for Nigerian culture prohibits young women from living alone in the city. Forced by the society to marry, Adah chooses Francis Obi, a quiet accounting student. Francis, however, is unable to pay the bride price and Adah's relatives refuse to attend her wedding. Nevertheless, Adah blossoms, giving birth to her first child and securing a lucrative position at the American Consulate. When the couple decides to emigrate to England in order to pursue higher education, however, Francis refuses to get a job, and Adah, who is pregnant with her third child, must work. She enrages Francis by using birth control and becomes a scapegoat for his academic failures. Still, the young wife steadfastly accepts her husband's shortcomings and becomes the confident wage-earning "man" of the family; simultaneously she begins to write her life's story. By creatively reconstructing her unhappy marriage, Adah begins to redefine herself. However, Francis burns her only manuscript, and Adah finally rejects the abusive marriage that was never validated by the payment of her bride price. In retaliation, Francis informs her that she is nothing more than an African woman living in poverty—a second-class citizen in England.

The Bride Price, published in 1976, continues to focus on Nigerian life. The thirteen-year-old heroine, Aku-nna, suffers the unexpected death of her beloved father and grows up in her uncle's household. She falls in love with a charismatic village schoolteacher who is an *osu*, or the descendant of a religious slave-cult. In order to save herself from being raped by a rival suitor, Aku-nna blatantly lies and declares she has already had sexual intercourse with her *osu* lover, Chike. Her uncle Okonkwo is enraged and refuses Chike's bride price because the union of Aku-nna and an *osu* violates Igbo law and defiles his family. The lovers reject their traditional culture, but their life together is short, for Aku-nna dies in childbirth. Not surprisingly, Aku-nna's tragic story becomes a village classic. Her fate reinforces the traditional beliefs that a woman may not choose her own husband, her bride price must be paid, and those who reject tradition are punished. Although this message is clear, the novel is ambiguous, for in the end Chike names his motherless child "Joy."

The Slave Girl, published in 1977, continues to present an ambiguous view of traditional life in a semi-autobiographical way. The story is inspired by the life of Emecheta's mother and focuses on a young woman who moves from one master to another in various dimensions of slavery. As a child in the village of Ibuza, Alice Ojebeta Ogbanje is orphaned and sold into slavery by her brothers for the sum of eight pounds. Her first owner is a powerful market woman, Ma Palagada, who sends young Ojebeta to the church mission school in the early days of colonialism. Although Ma Palagada's son Clifford proposes marriage, Ojebeta declines and is allowed to return to Ibuza. She marries Jacob, a hardworking, traditional Igbo who frees Ojebeta from the Palagada's control. However, upon her marriage Ojebeta kneels before her husband, accepting him as her new owner and master. Ojebeta is satisfied with her fate. She belongs to her husband, body and soul, and submits to his occasional beatings. She lives a life of slavery—a life she cannot change. Not only is she enslaved by her husband and society, she has tightened the noose around her neck by submitting to Christianity. Ojebeta is also named Ogbanje, the Igbo term for a changeling child who cannot sustain life and dies only to return to its mother's womb to be born and die again. The author's implication is that a woman's life is a continuous cycle of suffering and death. Nevertheless, her protagonist does not condemn this cycle of enslavement, for Alice Ojebeta Ogbanje is resigned to her designated lot in life.

In 1980, Emecheta published two works of fiction for young adults, *The Moonlight Bride* and *The Wrestling Match*. Both pieces are suspenseful and easy to read. In *The Moonlight Bride*, Ngbeke, a young Igbo girl, tells the story of a mysterious marriage. The village bustles with anticipation as youngsters craft new oil lamps and young men prepare a magnificent python-skin mat for the bride. The groom remains unknown until he is misunderstood and mistreated by his prospective kinsmen; the bride's identity is still a secret. However, the girls have heard that she is fair and full of good sense. Finally, the moonlight bride arrives, and Ngbeke and her friends are astonished, for she is an albino. Nevertheless, the village joyfully welcomes their new bride, and although she is different, she becomes a great asset to the community.

The Wrestling Match recounts a moral dilemma and focuses on Nigerian society in the aftermath of the civil war. Sixteen-year-old Okei Agiliga and many of his peers have lost their parents in the Biafran War. In fact, his age-group is called *Umu aya Biafra*, meaning all children born around the time of the civil war. Okei disdains farming and sits idle and troublesome in his uncle's village of Igbuno. Other disgruntled boys in the neighboring village of Akepi accuse Okei and his friends of stealing from their elders and disrupting village life. Tensions escalate and the rivals attempt to settle their differences in a wrestling match. However, tempers flare and the match disintegrates into a riot which only the elders can control. In the end, the young people learn that differences cannot be settled by brute force, for in war no one wins and everyone suffers.

Emecheta continues the theme of war in *Destination Biafra*, published in 1982, and presents a new kind of heroine. Debbie Ogedemgbe is a young educated woman who attempts to transcend the politics and violence of the Biafran War between 1966–1970. The story recounts the tensions among the Hausa and Igbo people, Biafra's declaration of independence, and the ensuing civil war. Debbie Ogedemgbe, an enlisted soldier, is sent on a peace mission to Biafra; however, she is illegally detained and brutally raped by Nigerian troops. She retreats to England, collects food for the starving Biafrans, and returns to Nigeria at the end of the war. Although Debbie tries to cross the lines of ethnicity and gender, she is violated as a woman soldier and perceived as a ploy in sexual politics. She declares her independence and refuses to marry her former lover, Alan Grey, a British politician. Like Nigeria, Debbie disengages herself from her former colonizer; she also vows to testify about the atrocities she has witnessed. Debbie's experience of the civil war focuses on women violated by men. This action serves as a microcosm of the civil war in which Nigeria was raped by her own people.

Double Yoke, published in 1982, is about Nko, another young woman studying at a Nigerian university who labors under both traditional and modern value systems—a doubly heavy, clumsy, and contradictory yoke. She desires to be both a loving wife and mother and a professional woman; however, neither traditional nor modern society accepts Nko. Her aggressive and jealous boyfriend, Ete Kamba, forces himself upon her and then becomes obsessed with fear that Nko may not have been a virgin before their sexual encounter. He confides in a spiritual advisor, the Reverend Professor Ikot, who dissuades him from his love affair and proceeds to seduce and eventually impregnate Nko himself. However, Nko realizes her dilemma and the injustices she faces. She chooses to turn a helpless situation into a sexual bargain. She rejects Ete and threatens to blackmail Ikot unless he ensures her a first-class honors degree. She vows to raise her child single-handedly and is determined to succeed professionally. However, the sudden death of her father shatters her plans, and she returns to her family in the village. Ironically, Ete joins her. The novel states that the educated Nigerian woman is expected to be both the submissive, docile female as well as a modern, sophisticated career women. However, these demands cause confusion for individuals, tensions between men and women, and a type of anomie or normlessness of gender in society. Ete's ambivalence toward Nko mirrors the hypocrisy of Nigerian society toward women; however, the ending of the novel suggests that Ete and Nko truly love one another and will attempt to bear their double yoke together—in her family's village, not in academia or in a modern urban center.

Emecheta further addresses the rape of African culture through the destruction of women in *The Rape of Shavi*, published in 1983. Despite the fact that Shavi is an idealized, mythical land inhabited by peaceloving and tolerant people, women are clitorized before they are married, and defective infants are eliminated through euthanasia. As a result, Shavi seems to be a flawless society. However, the moral fiber of the society seems to fray as King Patayon and his queen humiliate one another publicly, and the chief priest of the goddess Ogene claims divine authority. As the elders attempt to sort out the society's problems, an airplane carrying a group of Europeans attempting to escape a nuclear holocaust crashes in Shavi. The tragic drama unfolds, for the arrival of the uninvited visitors is symbolic of colonization. Although the survivors attempt to dialogue with their African hosts, they make no attempt to learn their language. Furthermore, while the Shavians evaluate the visitors' new ways, traditional life is destroyed. External pressure on the culture is symbolized as Ayoko, the wife of the crown prince Asogba, is raped by Ronje, a European intruder. Internal pressure resulting in the breakdown of the culture is symbolized by Asogba who assimilates European ways by waging war on neighboring kingdoms. The people of Shavi are destroyed as Asogba's wives contract syphilis and are unable to produce an heir. The novel focuses on the diametrically opposed languages of tradition and technology. The language of tradition is rooted in the grammar of myths, fables, and divine knowledge; the language of technology is rooted in the grammar of scientific knowledge. In this political parable, the weaknesses of the Shavian culture make it vulnerable to colonization; as Shavi disintegrates, it loses its voice and is drowned out by the language of the oppressor. Tragically, the peaceful Shavi is destroyed as a result of its encounter with the West.

Head Above Water, published in 1986, is Emecheta's autobiography. In this piece she discusses incidents she has elaborated on in *Second-Class Citizen*, *In the Ditch*, *The Bride Price*, *The Slave Girl*, *The Joys of Motherhood*, and *Double Yoke*. She also focuses on many specific events that have shaped her into a prolific and popular writer. The title refers to the miracle of her life's work—keeping her head above water—as a single mother of five children struggling to survive in London as a writer. Emecheta describes her transition from childhood in the rural areas of Nigeria to life as an internationally acclaimed author. She begins with the life of her mother, Alice Ogbanje Ojebeta Emecheta, a child orphaned during the First World War and sold into slavery by her brother. She then discusses her student days at the Methodist Girls High School and her marriage to Sylvester Onwordi at the age of sixteen. She depicts her struggles as a young mother, her pursuit of a degree in sociology, the disintegration of her marriage, her early career, her struggle to write, and her relationship with her publishers. Emecheta's autobiography is dedicated to the memory of her daughter Chiedu Onwordi, who died suddenly in May of 1984 at the age of twenty-three. This autobiography reveals Emecheta's determination and ability to balance many loads; overall, *Head Above Water* provides tremendous insight into the writer's life and spirit.

In 1989 Emecheta published a novel titled *Gwendolen*, which later appeared as *The Family*. This story recounts the life of a Jamaican family in England and focuses on a child who is left with her elderly grandmother, Naomi. Although she is a good child who works faithfully on the farm, at the age of eight, she is continually raped by a churchgoing friend of the family named Uncle Johnny. Eventually, the abused child is summoned to England by her parents who expect her to help with the housework and take care of her three younger siblings. Gwendolen attends a British school which soon becomes a place of humiliation and shame because she cannot read or write English. While her mother returns to Jamaica for a period of two years, Gwen turns her back on school and assumes the duties of a surrogate mother. Tragically, however, in a replay of her childhood horror, her father, Winston Brillianton, impregnates his daughter. As the pressure at home intensifies, Gwen finds herself in a mental institution and eventually becomes a ward of the state. Daddy Winston sinks deeper and deeper into despair and finally commits suicide at work. Never revealing his secret, Gwen gives birth to a beautiful child, whom she names "Iyamide," which means "my mother is here." Gwen is delighted with her daughter, who so clearly resembles her father, and looks to the future with hope and determination.

Like many of Emecheta's earlier novels, Kehinde, published in 1994, explores the dynamic relationships between Nigerian men and women in London and Lagos. The protagonist, Kehinde, whose name means "the twin who follows behind," seems to live two lives: in one she is confident and competent; in the other, she is depressed and marginalized. She embodies the chi of both her mother and twin who died in childbirth, and it is the spirit of her twin, Taiwo, "the one who tasted the world first," who assists her in making sound choices and living her life as a talented and independent person. Her husband, Albert, is happy in their monogamous London marriage; however, he insists upon the abortion of their third child in order to facilitate their return to Nigeria as a prosperous family who has "been to London and back." By fulfilling his dream of becoming a chief in his homeland, Albert actually becomes a symbol of oppression as he takes on second and third wives without Kehinde's consent. Wedging tradition between them, Albert alienates Kehinde, who leaves Nigeria a second time for London. She exchanges the charade of a "successful" man's senior wife and the burden of independently supporting her children for a meaningful position in the Department of Social Services and a new relationship with a man who respects her needs and human dignity. Like so many of Emecheta's other heroines, Kehinde speaks for women's rights in male dominated societies.

Resources
ALLAN, TUZYLINE JITA. "*The Joys of Motherhood*: A Study of a Problematic Womanist Aesthetic." In *Womanist and Feminist Aesthetics: A Comparative Review*, 95–117. Athens: Ohio University Press, 1995. A comparative analysis of Emecheta and other women writers.

AMADIUME, IFI. *Male Daughters, Female Husbands: Gender and Sex in an African Society*. Atlantic Highlands, N.J.: Zed Books, 1987. An anthropological study of an Igbo society indicating that gender is separate from biological sex, for women take on male roles acting as sons to their parents and husbands to other women.

BRUNNER, CHARLOTTE, ed. *The Heinemann Book of African Women's Writing*. Portsmouth, N.H.: Heinemann, 1993. An anthology representing western, eastern, northern, and southern African writings, including "Mother Was a Great Man" and two other Nigerian selections.

————. *Unwinding Threads: Writing by Women in Africa.* Portsmouth, N.H.: Heinemann, 1994. A popular collection of short stories and extracts from novels written by African women including selections from Ama Ata Aidoo, Mariama Ba, Flora Nwapa, and Buchi Emecheta.

CHIPSAULA, STELLA, and FRANK CHIPSAULA, eds. *The Heinemann Book of African Women's Poetry.* Portsmouth, N.H.: Heinemann, 1995. A collection of poetry written by women from Algeria, Egypt, Morocco, Tunisia, Benin, Ghana, Nigeria, São Tomé and Príncipe, Senegal, Kenya, Malawi, Mauritius, Uganda, Angola, Zambia, Mozambique, South Africa, and Zimbabwe.

DAVIES, CAROLE BOYCE. "Motherhood in the Works of Male and Female Igbo Writers: Achebe, Emecheta, Nwapa and Nzekwu." In *Ngambika: Studies of Women in African Literature,* 241–256. Trenton, N.J.: African World Press, 1986. A brief discussion of mother as slave in Emecheta's work and comparative analysis of the concept of motherhood.

FISHBURN, KATHERINE. *Reading Buchi Emecheta: Cross-Cultural Conversations.* Westport, Conn.: Greenwood Press, 1995. A close reading of many of Emecheta's novels with particular attention to problematic elements for western feminist readers.

FRANK, KATHERINE. "Women Without Men: The Feminist Novel in Africa." In Eldred Jones, ed., *Women in African Literature Today,* 14–34. Trenton, N.J.: Africa World Press, 1987. An insightful discussion of *Double Yoke* and *Destination Biafra* as well as other novels written by African women.

IMAM, A., et al. *Women and the Family in Nigeria.* Dakar, Senegal: Council for the Development of Economic and Social Research in Africa, 1989. A volume organized by "Women in Nigeria" in 1982 covering various topics including work and family, reproduction, religion, and literature.

ISICHEI, ELIZABETH. *A History of the Igbo People.* New York: St. Martin's Press, 1976. A basic history of Igboland from prehistoric times through the colonial period and its aftermath, with an interesting section on the Women's War of 1929–30.

JAMES, ADEOLA. "Buchi Emecheta." In *In Their Own Voices: African Women Writers Talk,* 34–45. Portsmouth, N.H.: Heinemann, 1990. An interview with Emecheta conducted in London in 1986.

NWAPA, FLORA. *Efuru.* Portsmouth, N.H.: Heinemann, 1966. A complex tale about a talented, wealthy, and beautiful Igbo woman who cannot conceive and never experiences the joy of motherhood.

OGUNDIPE-LESLIE, MOLARA. "The Female Writer and Her Commitment." In Eldred Jones, ed., *Women in African Literature Today,* 5–13. Trenton, N.J.: Africa World Press, 1987. A general discussion of the role and responsibilities of the female writer.

OGUNYEMI, CHIKWENYE OKONJO. *African Wo/Man Palava: The Nigerian Novel by Women.* Chicago: University of Chicago Press, 1996. An interesting collection of essays on Nigerian women writers including an overview of Flora Nwapa and Buchi Emecheta's work.

OHADIKE, DON C. *Anioma: A Social History of the Western Igbo People.* Athens: Ohio University Press, 1994. An interesting discussion of women's associations and food production among women of the Anioma area of Igboland.

OKONJO, KAMENE. "Women's Political Participation in Nigeria." In Filomina Steady, ed. *The Black Woman Cross-Culturally,* 79–106. Cambridge, Mass.: Schenkman Books, 1985. A review of Igbo women's traditional political institutions and their disintegration during the colonial period.

ORGANIZATION OF AMERICAN HISTORIANS. *Restoring Women to History: Teaching Packets for Integrating Women's History into Courses on Africa, Asia, Latin America, The Caribbean and the Middle East.* Bloomington, In.: Organization of American Historians, 1988. A practical guide for teaching women's history with an overview of research on African women ranging from ancient times to the twentieth century.

PHILLIPS, MAGGI. "Engaging Dreams: Alternative Perspectives on Flora Nwapa, Buchi Emecheta, Ama Ata Aidoo, Bessie Head, and Tsitsi Dangarembga's Writing." In *Research in African Literatures* 25, 4 (Winter 1994): 89–103. A discussion of supernatural directives in *The Joys of Motherhood* and other novels by African women.

SENGUPTA, SHIVAJI. "Desire and The Politics of Control in *The Joys of Motherhood* and *The Family.*" In Marie Umeh, ed., *Emerging Perspectives on Buchi Emecheta*, 227–249. Trenton, N.J.: Africa World Press, 1996. An analysis of the two protagonists who desire freedom yet are destroyed by the ideals of womanhood created by men.

UCHENDU, VICTOR C. *The Igbo of Southeast Nigeria.* New York: Holt, Rinehart and Winston, 1965. A basic anthropological case study of the Igbo people including a discussion of religion, customs, government, and family.

UMEH, MARIE. "Procreation, Not Recreation: Decoding Mama in Buchi Emecheta's *The Joys of Motherhood.*" In *Emerging Perspectives on Buchi Emecheta*, 190–206. Trenton, N.J.: Africa World Press, 1996. An analysis of cultural codes and feminist expressions protesting the Igbo's oppression of women—an injustice which destroys feminine sexual desire.

———. "Reintegration with the Lost Self: A Study of Buchi Emecheta's *Double Yoke.*" In Carol Boyce Davies, ed., *Ngambika: Studies of Women in African Literature*, 173–180. Trenton, N.J.: Africa World Press, 1986. A discussion of Nko, which provides insight into the psyche of modern African women.

———, ed. *Emerging Perspectives on Buchi Emecheta.* Trenton, N.J.: Africa World Press, 1996. A comprehensive review of Emecheta's work by a variety of critics including an introduction which locates sexual politics within Igbo society.

WIPPER, AUDREY. "Women's Voluntary Associations." In Margaret Jean Hay, ed., *African Women South of the Sahara*, 69–86. New York: Longman, 1984. A discussion of African women's groups with a section on the Igbo women's custom of "sitting on a man" or "making war."

A Selected Bibliography of Buchi Emecheta's Work

In the Ditch. London: Barrie and Jenkins, 1972; Portsmouth, N.H.: Heinemann, 1994.

Second-Class Citizen. London: Allison and Busby, 1974; New York: George Braziller, 1975.

The Bride Price. London: Allison and Busby, 1976; New York: George Braziller, 1976.

The Slave Girl. London: Allison and Busby, 1977; New York: George Braziller, 1977.

The Joys of Motherhood. London: Allison and Busby, 1979; Portsmouth, N.H.: Heinemann, 1994.

The Moonlight Bride. London: Oxford University Press, 1980; New York: George Braziller, 1983.

The Wrestling Match. London: Oxford University Press, 1980; New York: George Braziller, 1983.

Destination Biafra. London: Allison and Busby, 1982; Portsmouth, N.H.: Heinemann, 1994.

Double Yoke. London: Ogwugwu Afo, 1982; New York: George Braziller, 1983.

The Rape of Shavi. London: Ogwugwu Afo, 1983; New York: George Braziller, 1985.

Head Above Water. London: Ogwugwu Afo, 1986; Portsmouth, N.H.: Heinemann, 1994.

The Family. Originally published as *Gwendolen*. London: Winston Collins and Sons, 1989; New York: George Braziller, 1990.

Kehinde. Portsmouth, N.H: Heinemann, 1994.

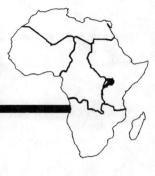

UGANDA

Okot p'Bitek satirizes society in *Song of Lawino* and *Song of Ocol* in an adaption of the traditional Acholi song story. The Acholi people inhabit the northern areas of Uganda.

Chapter 3

Okot p'Bitek and Song of Lawino *and* Song of Ocol

Okot p'Bitek is a biting satirist who sparked a literary revolution in East Africa soon after Uganda gained her independence. He is best known for the traditional African woman's lament in *Song of Lawino* and her westernized husband's response in *Song of Ocol*. *Song of Lawino*, which was originally written in Acholi and later translated into English, was published in 1966. *Song of Ocol* was written as a response to Lawino's lament and was published in 1970. These two songs were later republished in a single volume. The narratives reflect the traditional song stories of the Acholi people and raise issues concerning the conflict of culture. Both songs dramatize the tension between the values and lifestyles of traditional Acholi people and the new educated elite who seek to imitate western civilization. The tension is heightened as it is articulated by husband and wife. Lawino berates her husband Ocol for uprooting the pumpkin, or the traditions of the Acholi people; Ocol responds with disdain.

Song of Lawino and *Song of Ocol* are suitable for students on the lower or intermediate levels. Because *Song of Ocol* is a response to the first narrative, it cannot stand on its own. Both songs are excellent examples of satire and provide opportunities for students to dramatize both sides of the culture clash.

Song of Lawino, Song of Ocol, and the Acholi People of Uganda

Song of Lawino and *Song of Ocol* are two separate narratives written in lyrical verse about distinct fictional characters. The first song exposes a traditional Acholi woman's conflict with her westernized husband; the second song is the husband's response to his wife's bitter complaint. Lawino champions traditional African culture and life while Ocol defends the changes introduced by colonialism. Both Lawino and Ocol are like caricatures in a melodrama, yet each song echoes the traditional Acholi oral song performance.

The first two sections of *Song of Lawino* introduce the fictional situation of the narrative. In the sections that follow, Lawino compares concrete elements of Acholi life such as dances, ornaments, and hairstyles with new European ways. In the later sections, she addresses more abstract subjects such as time, Christianity, mission education, western medicine, and the new politics of independence. Finally, she sums up her argument with extended metaphors. Overall, Lawino's song is addressed to her husband, Ocol; however, she also takes her dilemma to the center of the Acholi compound. She asks the community and the reader to sympathize with her and affirm her belief in the value of traditional life.

In her introduction, Lawino explains how her husband has rejected her as primitive and inhuman and how he has replaced traditional ways with the modern, progressive, and supposedly civilized ways of the white man. She then focuses on Clementine, an African woman, who like Ocol seeks to negate her African nature and make herself white. A simile compares Clementine's lips to red-hot coals and a metaphor compares the wigged woman to a powdered guinea fowl. Lawino also introduces a proverb which captures the essence of her argument and is repeated throughout her lament. She states: "The pumpkin in the old homestead must not be uprooted!" The pumpkin is a durable vegetable which historically sustained the people through famine. Planted with great ceremony, its flowers give the homestead the assurance of survival, and it stands as a kind of anchor for the people ensuring stability in society. Lawino begs her husband not to uproot the pumpkin, for ripping out the roots of tradition will destroy the homestead.

In sections three through six, Lawino focuses on concrete elements of life and praises herself in contrast to her rival. She celebrates the beautiful dances of the Acholi which boast the gracefulness of the human body in the traditional dance arenas, and she rejects the obscene European ballroom dances where shameless partners hold one another in public as they kiss and suck each other's saliva. Lawino reminisces about attracting her husband with her dancing as the young leader of the girls and compares herself to the graceful giraffe who simply cannot become an ugly monkey like Clementine. She defends herself and her way of life, including her traditional methods of grinding grain and cooking on the three-stoned fireplace.

In sections seven through eleven, Lawino satirizes abstract concepts of westernized life. She complains about her husband's time-ticking clock which she cannot read and which she does not need, for she knows when it is time to feed the children and time to harvest the crops. She also claims ignorance of the good clean word in the missionaries' Bible and rejects Christians, who drink human blood from a sacrificial altar. Furthermore, she satirizes the priests and ministers who, like Ocol, are unable to answer her philosophical questions by claiming that the Acholi language is inadequate for expressing metaphysical concepts. Lawino also quarrels with Ocol over hygiene and western medicine and finds his disdain for traditional diviners, priests, and healers incomprehensible. Finally, she questions the new politics of independence which promises to unite the Acholi, Lango, Madi, Lugbara, Alur, Iteso, Baganda, Banyankole, and Banyoro peoples with the Jo-pa-Dhola and Toro peoples overnight in one independent and peaceful Uganda.

Lawino sums up her argument in an extended metaphor and plea for Ocol's purification in the last two sections of her lament. She appeals to her clansmen in an apostrophe and refers to her husband as a prince of the ancient chiefdom who has lost his mind through western education. He is worthless, for his manhood is destroyed; his testicles have been smashed with heavy schoolbooks in the colonial oppressor's classroom. Yet, Lawino still holds out hope for Ocol's recovery. He is the son of the Bull, a brave and respected leader, and he can still be purified by begging for forgiveness and receiving a new spear symbolizing sexual prowess and strength. Then he will be freed from his emasculation at the hands of the white man. As his first wife, the one who loves him and cares for him like a mother, Lawino begs Ocol to let her dance for him once more and show him the richness of African life. She begs her husband to love her again and to refrain from uprooting the life-giving pumpkin of tradition.

Ocol will have none of it! He begins *Song of Ocol* by telling Lawino to shut up, pack her things, and go. His narrative is shorter and in direct response to Lawino's lament, and therefore it cannot stand on its own. Basically, Ocol rejects Lawino's song about tradition, reveals his disdain of Africa and himself, ridicules the people of Africa, and looks to other members of the neocolonial elite for a new way of life.

Ocol uses several similes to reject Lawino's song. He claims her lament is a solitary cry without a chorus and compares it to the confused death-noise of a butchered ram. He compares her song to rotting buffalo meat abandoned by poachers to provide a feast for pests and scavengers like pus-filled maggots, bald-headed vultures, and snarling hyenas. Furthermore, he clearly states that the pumpkin of tradition will not only be uprooted, it will be obliterated—an image he refers to repeatedly throughout his song.

After ordering his houseboy to cleanse his home upon Lawino's departure, he reveals that Africa is nothing but deep unfathomable darkness for him. In despair, Ocol wonders why he was born into this void, and why he was born black. Attempting to right this wrong, he vows to destroy tradition in every form. All ancient taboos will be smashed, all sacred trees will be demolished, and all the traditional leaders of Africa will be destroyed. Village poets, musicians, dancers, and storytellers will be silenced, and teachers of African history will be shunned. All African statesmen will be thrown into detention, and Ocol will not look back to the blackness of his past.

Everything connected with traditional life must be destroyed. Ocol begs the women of Africa to smash the water pots they carry which symbolize their oppression and degradation, and he continues to rant about the primitive ethnic groups of East Africa. He disparages all African people ranging from the elders of Karamojong to the mighty warriors of Maasailand, claiming that these ignorant men simply defend barren empires that are closed to progress. Furthermore, he promises that as the elders, who are the guardians of traditions, are arrested, a select few young people will be invited into the new Africa.

Ocol completes his song with an all-encompassing denunciation of Africa. He vows that every tree sacred to every African ethnic group will be uprooted; he promises that great mountains like Kilimanjaro will be blown up, and the mighty waters of the Nile will be diverted into the Indian Ocean. As he sings the funeral dirge for the old homestead, he salutes the ministers of a new order—the new head of state, the black bishop, the fat black capitalists, and all the architects and engineers of a modern nation. As concrete and steel underpin the new city, monuments will be erected to honor the butchers of Africa including Leopold of Belgium, and streets will commemorate those great discoverers of African life such as David Livingstone and Henry Stanley. Ocol's final wish is that the great chiefs and kings of Africa's ancient empires rot in their graves. He shakes his head and wonders what kind of a poem one could possibly write for these, the vanquished peoples of the earth.

The songs of Lawino and Ocol echo the clash of cultures as European powers colonized the peoples of Uganda. Lawino represents the Acholi people who inhabit the northern region of Uganda, and Ocol champions the culture of the Europeans. The Acholi are a subgroup of the Luo people of the southern Sudan, and have developed a culture closely related to other Luo groups in East Africa. The Acholi developed an economy based on agriculture and animal husbandry and cultivated a variety of crops including the drought-resistant pumpkin and a wide assortment of beans. The family remained the central unit of social organization, and related lineages combined to form clans which were headed by elders with ritual authority. Each clan inhabited a particular area, controlled a specific hunting ground, owned ancestral shrines, and organized communal work on common lands.

The Acholi clans were loosely organized under the *rwot*, or chief, who was a central figure with ritual, judicial, executive, and legislative powers. He was the link between the living and dead and offered sacrifices to the ancestors on behalf of the people. All clans in a chiefdom paid tribute to the *rwot*, sought his protection against enemies, and respected his authority in settling disputes with other clans. The *rwot* was entitled to labor from every clan and held his position through the general consent of the clans under his jurisdiction; consequently, disputes among clans caused many subgroups to develop.

The nineteenth century introduced profound changes among the people of East Africa. In the early 1820s, the Arab slave traders saw northern Uganda as a potential source of ivory and slaves. They conquered the Luo easily and called the people "Shuli," a term which was translated by other invaders as "Acholi" or "Acoli." The slave and ivory trade flourished until 1871 when Sir Samuel Baker arrived and attempted to curtail the slave traders in the Acholi area. Explorers such as David Livingstone and Henry Stanley soon followed searching for the source of the Nile River.

Uganda was declared a British protectorate in 1894, and the colonial administration gradually imposed its rule throughout the region. In 1913 the British appointed chiefs who took over the leadership of lineages, clans, and chiefdoms; these new chiefs also collected taxes for the British and attempted to settle disputes about ownership of the land. The old system of political authority and social organization marked by consent was dismantled and replaced by a new system of authoritarian and centralized government.

In 1904 the first Christian reading house was established in Acholiland and chiefs were invited to send sons to learn reading, mathematics, and catechism. The first permanent Anglican Church Mission Society station was set up in Gulu in 1913, and within several years teachers were dispatched throughout Acholiland. The Roman Catholic White Fathers and Verona Fathers soon followed and established competing reading houses. Through their ignorance of the traditional religion and the Acholi language, the missionaries forced the Acholi to adopt the concept of Lubanga to represent the Christian creator God. However, Lubanga actually referred to death, evil incarnate, and Satan in the traditional world view and was the antithesis of the Acholi supreme god named Jok; thus, Christianity forced the people to invert ideological concepts of good and evil. In addition, many of the Protestant and Catholic converts were openly hostile to each other as they developed new religious allegiances which cut across clan and chiefdom loyalties.

As the missionaries introduced a new religion, the colonial administration attempted to develop a new economy. Cotton was introduced as a cash crop which would provide the Acholi with money to pay taxes and school fees. Overall, however, farming was difficult, and Acholiland offered no other economic opportunities. As a result, young men migrated to the southern areas of the protectorate where they served in the colonial police or armed forces and fought for the British in Burma during World War II. Many Acholi also served in the Fourth King's African Rifles Battalion, which fought against the Mau Mau freedom fighters in Kenya in the early 1950s.

After World War II, the political consciousness of the veterans resulted in several political parties that paved the way for independence. The Ugandan National Congress was formed by educated Protestants from Buganda; the Progressive Party appealed to conservative Baganda intellectuals; and the Democratic Party attracted Baganda and Acholi Catholics who opposed Protestant control. Needless to say, the spirit of nationalism did not readily emerge among the forty distinct ethnic groups who spoke thirty-two different languages in Uganda. The British had encouraged enmity among the people by granting the Baganda people privileged status and developing the resources of the south while treating the Acholi in the north as a reservoir of migrant labor. As the wealthy Buganda people attempted to establish a separate independent state, ethnic divisions and religious differences were underscored. Nevertheless, in 1960 Milton Obote formed the Uganda People's Congress in a deeply divided Uganda. Although the 1961 election was boycotted by the Baganda, Obote led the peoples of Uganda to a tenuous independence from Britain in October 1962.

Literary Techniques in **Song of Lawino** *and* **Song of Ocol**

Song of Lawino reflects the impact of colonialism. Lawino herself uses many traditional literary techniques of the Acholi song story such as African images, repetition, similes, symbols, metaphors, proverbs, lampoons, and apostrophes to plead her case and involve her audience. Ocol does not employ the traditional literary techniques as faithfully as Lawino as he attempts to defend himself and the destruction of traditional Africa.

For example, Lawino uses traditional images to criticize Clementine, saying:

> The beautiful one aspires
> To look like a white woman;
>
> Her lips are red-hot
> Like glowing charcoal,
> She resembles the wild cat
> That has dipped its mouth in blood. . . . (p. 37)

Lawino also uses repetition of phrases to pound her point home to Ocol as she describes him making love with Clementine:

> You kiss her on the cheek
> As white people do,
> You kiss her open-sore lips
> As white people do,
> You suck the slimy saliva
> From each other's mouths
> As white people do. (p. 44)

Lawino uses a variety of similes and metaphors describing Clementine, saying:

> The beautiful one is dead dry
> Like a stump,
> She is meatless
> Like a shell
> On a dry river bed. (p. 40)

Lawino also employs symbols representing traditional life, using the horn, bull, and spear to lament her husband's loss of traditional qualities. The horn is not only a musical instrument but also a ritual object connected with initiation into adulthood. Acholi men blew their horns as a signal of individuality and reputation. The bull represents bravery and respect, and Lawino combines the symbols of the bull and horn to remind Ocol of the famous ancestry from which he descends. The spear symbolizes the essence of manhood in the Acholi culture, for a man is never buried without his spear. Using the spear as a phallic symbol, Lawino ridicules Ocol's impotence and alienation from tradition. She insists that he must ask for a new spear to restore his manhood.

The symbol of the pumpkin, which represents Acholi culture and traditional values, is repeated in a refrain from an Acholi proverb that ties the entire narrative together. Throughout her song Lawino cries:

> The pumpkin in the old homestead
> Must not be uprooted! (p. 41)

Lawino presses her point, insisting that neither Clementine nor Ocol can become white westerners, with another proverb saying:

> The long-necked and graceful giraffe
> Cannot become a monkey. (p. 56)

Finally, Lawino uses a lampoon to indict her husband saying:

> You may not feel so,
> But you behave like
> A dog of the white man!
> . . . The dogs of white men
> Are well trained
> And they understand English! (p. 115)

Lawino concludes her song with an apostrophe pleading her case with the Acholi community, saying:

> O, my clansmen,
> Let us all cry together!
> Come,
> Let us mourn the death of my
>   husband. . . . (p. 116)

**LAWINO BEGS OCOL NOT TO UPROOT THE PUMPKIN IN THE OLD
HOMESTEAD.**

Points to Ponder

The character of Lawino may be a fictionalization of Okot p'Bitek's
mother, the great storyteller Lacwaa Cerina. Whether Lawino was inspired
by a real person or not, she has provoked much debate in literary circles. Is
Lawino credible? Does she truly represent the women of East Africa, or is
she a caricature, a gross exaggeration of the true African woman? Is Lawino
a pathetic portrait of a stupid wife scorned by her progressive husband? Is
she blindly clutching the past and offering ridiculous comparisons between
Acholi customs and western changes? How does Lawino compare herself to
Clementine? How is the reader to understand the sections where Lawino
appears foolish? Has the author effectively captured the female voice, or is
the song an abomination of the African woman? And what about Ocol,
who is berated for uprooting the traditions of the Acholi people? By adopt-
ing the values of the colonial oppressors and shunning traditional life, has he
betrayed his community and disgraced his ancestors? Has Ocol truly lost his

manhood in a forest of white men's books, or is he pursuing a better life? How do you feel about Lawino as she pleads with Ocol to come back to his senses, to recognize the value of traditional life, and to love her again?

Although Lawino and Ocol each defends a particular way of life, do they also deny themselves? Ocol not only detests Lawino, who can neither read nor write, but he despises Africa and all that is African. Tantamount to his betrayal of his people, he despises himself and deplores the very color of his own skin. He praises the colonial imperialists who raped Africa, and he is proud to be a rich neocolonial elite who takes absolutely no responsibility for improving the economic plight of the rural peasants. Does Lawino likewise simultaneously defend and detest herself and her way of life?

Furthermore, is the exchange between Lawino and Ocol actually a dialogue between tradition and change? If so, where does the author, Okot p'Bitek, stand in the debate? As an educated, westernized Acholi writing shortly after Uganda gained her independence, which character does he use as his spokesperson—Lawino or Ocol? Is the author saying that the change represented by Ocol will not only destroy traditional Acholi life but will also destroy postcolonial Uganda? Does the author wish to live life with Lawino?

Another discussion may focus on the relationship of the two narratives to traditional Acholi songs. In what ways do the songs reflect the song stories of the Acholi? Can students bring the narratives to life by dramatizing the conflict between Lawino and Ocol and interact with their audience as the Acholi singer would? Inspired by *Song of Lawino* and *Song of Ocol*, can students write their own songs to satirize current issues using a variety of literary techniques? A more in-depth understanding of the traditional Acholi song is helpful in addressing these issues.

Traditional Acholi Songs and Dances
The Acholi people of Uganda in East Africa value storytelling as an important art. Performing stories through dance and telling stories through song are crucial didactic methods of retelling history, defining social norms, instilling moral values, and venting individual differences. In the past, traditional dances ranged from formal communal celebrations dramatizing the power of the chiefdom, to trysts between groups of lovers. Stories included the family folklore shared around the evening fire as well as critical oral songs performed by professional singers in conjunction with a specific audience.

Traditionally, the Acholi retold their history and defined social norms through a variety of different dances. The *otole* songs and dances involved the whole community and were performed during elaborate political occasions; by reenacting past battles and retelling the exploits of war, the *otole* dance cemented relationships between two chiefdoms. Likewise, the *bwole* dance, which was often performed at coronations, further celebrated the power of the chief and his lineage. The *orak* dance was a popular dance between young people from neighboring clans who gathered together in the hopes of meeting a future spouse. Other songs and dances celebrated the hunt, prepared warriors for battle, and commemorated the dead through funeral dirges.

In addition to this dramatic communal story dancing, stories were performed regularly before responsive and participatory audiences. An evening in the family compound often began with children's stories; gradually the tales became longer and more complicated, addressing profound problems in the society. Often the storyteller proposed changes in the character and behavior of his audience and directed his lessons toward specific individuals. Although the basic tale may have been told many times before, each performance allowed the individual storyteller to recreate a unique story specific to a particular time, place, and situation.

In addition, oral songs were performed by professional singers who often accompanied themselves on musical instruments. These singers often integrated traditional myths into their songs and used a variety of techniques to point out undesirable traits in their listeners. The *carolok*, or proverb, was often used to allude to fact and give authority to the story's argument. The *calo*, or simile, created images that expressed exaggerated feelings ranging from admiration to disgust. Moreover, the singer often employed an apostrophe, whereby the audience was addressed and invited to respond. Often the apostrophe introduced dramatic confrontations between the singer and audience and provided a dramatic framework for the narrative. All these storytelling techniques underscored the social and moral norms which governed society. The dramatic interactive nature of the oral song emphasized responsibility to the society and allowed the individual and group to respond to the singer's criticism. Consequently, each story song was unique. Although a singer began with a basic story line, as he interacted with the audience, each performance took on a life of its own.

The Author and His Work

Okot p'Bitek

Okot p'Bitek was born in 1931 in the northern part of Uganda, and throughout his childhood both his parents kept the traditional Acholi folklore alive. His father, Opii Jebedyo, and his mother, Lacwaa Cerina, were members of the Patiko and Palaro chiefdoms in northern Acholiland and were attracted to the missionary activity of the Anglican Church Mission Society (CMS). Opii left his family's homestead at Ajulu and traveled fifteen miles south to Gulu, where he became a teacher at the CMS mission station. Opii often performed story songs around the evening fire, and Lacwaa, an accomplished composer and singer in her own right, inspired her son's interest in traditional oral literature.

As a bright and creative student, p'Bitek enjoyed a prestigious education yet maintained his interest in traditional music and literature. He attended Gulu High School and Kings College Budo. Here he wrote and produced an opera in English titled *Acan* about a poor slave boy who could not afford to marry his beloved. He then attended a teachers' training course at the Government Training College in Mbarara and taught for three years at Sir Samuel Baker's School near Gulu. While there he served as choirmaster and married his first wife, Anek. At the age of twenty-two, p'Bitek published his first novel in Acholi titled *Lak Tar Miyo Kinyero Wi Lobo*, or *Are Your Teeth White? Then Laugh!*

P'Bitek was an outstanding educator with diverse talents. In 1958 he was selected to play on the Ugandan national football team and tour Britain. He remained in England as a student and earned a certificate in education from Bristol University, a bachelor of laws degree cum laude from the University of Wales in Aberystwyth, and a bachelor of letters degree at the Institute of Social Anthropology in Oxford. His thesis focused on the social function of myths and proverbs, and analyzed the structure, style, and content of traditional Acholi songs.

In 1963, Okot p'Bitek returned to Uganda and joined the staff of the Extra-Mural Department at Makerere University. This position allowed him to expand his research on oral literature in northern Uganda. He also founded and organized the annual Gulu Festival of the Arts and married his second wife, Auma Kalina Kireng. During this time, p'Bitek wrote a song titled "Wer pa Lawino" in Acholi. The song was performed and discussed throughout the Gulu area, and in 1965 p'Bitek read a small section of the piece at the East African Cultural Heritage conference held in Nairobi. His song about Lawino was like an explosion that opened up the East African literary scene, for the traditional Acholi oral song was uniquely African and not structured after European models. Lawino's message about the value of African culture also challenged writers who looked to Europe for inspiration. P'Bitek published *Song of Lawino* in English in 1966 with the East African Publishing House; it soon became an East African classic.

At this time, p'Bitek was also appointed director of the Uganda National Theatre and Cultural Center in Kampala. Here he focused on rediscovering the richness of the various indigenous Ugandan cultures. He established a national choir, developed a puppet theatre, set up a permanent art exhibition, and sponsored regular weekly dance sessions organized by the Heartbeat of Africa troupe. The cultural activities culminated in a festival which lasted eight days and coincided with the independence celebrations in October 1967. Over 7,000 people participated in the festival which included songs, dramas, community dances, children's plays, and traditional games played in nearby villages. Soon after the festival, however, p'Bitek was abruptly dismissed from the center, most probably due to his explicit and extreme criticism of politicians in the postcolonial regime. He then took a position at Nairobi University in Kenya, where he continued to encourage local artists, and organized the first Kisumu Art Festival in 1968. He was later awarded research fellowships at the University of Iowa and the Institute of African Studies in Nairobi and taught at the University of Nairobi until 1978.

P'Bitek wrote steadily throughout his career. In 1970, he published *Song of Ocol* in response to Lawino's lament. This was followed by two important scholarly texts: *African Religions and Western Scholarship* (1970) and *Religion of the Central Luo* (1971). In 1971 he published *Song of Malaya* and *Song of Prisoner* in a volume entitled *Two Songs*, which won the Kenyatta Prize for Literature. *Africa's Cultural Revolution*, a collection of essays he had written and published in various journals over the course of many years, was published in 1973. *Horn of My Love*, a collection of Acholi songs, appeared in 1974, and in 1978, he published *Hare and Hornbill*, a collection of Acholi folktales.

P'Bitek also held visiting appointments at both the University of Texas at Austin and the University of Ife in Nigeria. After Idi Amin was overthrown in 1979, p'Bitek returned to the Institute of Social Research at Makerere University. In February 1982, he was appointed as the first professor of creative writing in the department of literature. Tragically, however, five months later, p'Bitek died at his home in Kampala at the age of fifty-one. Okot p'Bitek's premature death was a shock and tremendous loss for Uganda. His creative voice never ceased singing about Africa's rich cultural heritage, and he insisted that African literature be understood as a living social art. Today his work still challenges storytellers, singers, and writers to prick needles into their audiences and sing songs that will create just societies.

Okot p'Bitek's Work

Okot p'Bitek dedicated his professional teaching career, his writing, and his life to celebrating the culture of Africa. Throughout his work, he encouraged countless artists and expanded the concept of literature from the written word to include the sung and spoken word. Above all, he captured the essence of the Acholi oral song by translating this dynamic performance into a unique narrative form. Combining the traditional roles of storyteller and singer with the contemporary roles of writer and social critic, Okot p'Bitek's collections of Acholi songs and folklore preserve the literature of the past, and his scholarly work provides insight into African traditional religions.

In 1953 Okot p'Bitek wrote *Lak Tar Miyo Kinyero Wi Lobo*, or *Are Your Teeth White? Then Laugh!* Recently the novel has been published as *Lak Tar. White Teeth.* The hero is Okeca Ladwong, and the title reflects the nickname of Okeca's father. This nickname comes from an Acholi proverb which states, "Our teeth are white, that is why we laugh at the sorrows of the world." Although Okeca loses his father and faces desperate poverty, the proverb reminds him that sorrow should not weigh him down. As a member of his uncle's household, he does not inherit the funds required to pay the bride price of his beloved Cecilia. Therefore, like many other Acholi men who were unable to secure employment in the police force or army, Okeca migrates to Kampala where he lives in crowded conditions and works in the Jinja sugar plantations. Although the workers are bonded to stay for five years, Okeca helps a friend escape. He is later betrayed and demoted to heavy work. Finding his personal dilemma more painful than his financial woes, he too escapes the plantation. However, on his way home, his luggage and money are stolen, and the pitiful, forlorn Okeca walks back to Acholiland, destitute. Okeca's sad story reflects the economic situation of the Acholi people in the 1950s.

In 1971, Okot p'Bitek wrote *Song of Prisoner* and *Song of Malaya,* which were published in one volume entitled *Two Songs. Song of Prisoner* is explosive, focusing on the tragic elements of independence and the plight of ordinary African people at the hands of bloodthirsty dictators. This controversial piece was published about the time of Idi Amin's coup and provoked much controversy and political debate throughout East Africa. The song is dedicated to Patrice Lumumba, the idealist and charismatic leader of the independent Congo who was assassinated by African rebels in the early 1960s. As the song reflects his tragic demise, it symbolizes the decay and destruction of independent African nations.

The prisoner begins with a lament, for he has been brutally beaten and thrown into prison for vagrancy. As a victim of injustice and oppression, he cries of hunger, broods over his starving family, and attacks his captors and ancestors. He is overcome with a desire to drink human blood, eat human liver, and smear human fat all over his body. However, the audience soon realizes that the prisoner is actually a political assassin who, out of love for his country, killed a dictatorial, treasonous, and murderous head of state. The prisoner makes a morbid appeal to escape into total debauchery. He wishes to dance and fornicate his way into oblivion, for he sees himself as totally insignificant, a branch of the African tree of life which has been broken by the whirlwind of *uhuru*, or freedom. The prisoner's voice is a medley which may include voices from other cell blocks, and his audience appears to be a group of wardens who are generally unresponsive. His message is both pathetic and ambiguous—in some ways it reflects independent Africa, where the ordinary person is confused by military regimes, political assassins, and guerrilla freedom-fighters.

The morbid tone of *Song of Prisoner,* however, finds comic relief in *Song of Malaya,* the story of a good-natured prostitute who is proud of her profession and uniquely qualified to satirize East African society. Malaya's audience is a group of fellow prostitutes whom she encourages as she attacks society's norms and two-faced hypocrites. Malaya mocks the deceitful nature of the policeman who sleeps with her by night and arrests her by day; she satirizes the member of Parliament who simultaneously passes a slum clearance law and arranges the services of prostitutes after the social development project is complete. She rebukes the chief who accuses her of infecting him with venereal disease and mocks his unhappy wife. Malaya also denounces the priest and schoolmaster who preach monogamy and morality and call her children bastards. Even her own brother despises her as he simultaneously pays for the favors of other prostitutes. Malaya celebrates the universality of sexual desire experienced by every member of society from frustrated soldiers to rural engineers to city taxi drivers. By accepting all and refusing none, she acts as society's equalizer. Her monologue reveals her understanding of natural desire and asserts the moral superiority of her unorthodox life. The reader finds prostitution an honest profession compared with politics, law enforcement, teaching, the priesthood, or even marriage. Because she is completely unpretentious, Malaya seems to be psychologically and spiritually healthier than those who condemn her. Her message is acceptance of all that is natural, and she is completely tolerant of diversity.

In addition, Okot p'Bitek has collected Acholi games and songs in *Horn of My Love,* published in 1974, and Acholi folklore and stories in *Hare and Hornbill,* published in 1978. *Horn of My Love* contributes to the cultural and literary revolution in East Africa by collecting the lullabies, love songs, satirical verses, religious chants, war songs, and funeral dirges of the Acholi people. The author's purpose is to preserve Acholi traditional life, humor, and moral values. The first section describes children's games, dances, and occasions when various songs are sung. A description of the *orak,* the love dance; the *otole,* the war dance; and the funeral dances are included. Part two consists of the actual texts of the songs, satirical verses, and dirges in both Acholi and English. Part three contains various essays including an analysis of the themes presented in Acholi dirges, a discussion of the role of poets as historians, an explanation of the *mwoc,* or praise name, and finally, an exposition of various warrior titles.

Similarly, *Hare and Hornbill* is a fascinating collection of Acholi folklore. A clever rabbit and his animal friends take on human characteristics and in-

teract freely with men and women in order to explain natural phenome-
non, such as why the hyena is so ugly and why people must swat tsetse flies.
Other stories teach lessons and reinforce the moral code of society. Some
stories stress the consequences of foolishness and the importance of family
relationships while other tales retell the myths of creation and migration.
The history, fantasy, and satire of *Hare and Hornbill* reveal important aspects
of Acholi society and provide entertaining lessons for all.

In addition to fiction, Okot p'Bitek has wrestled with issues concerning African traditional religions in two scholarly works. In *African Religions
in Western Scholarship*, originally published in 1970, p'Bitek criticizes western
theological approaches which perceive African societies as either grotesque
and wild or nobly savage and innocent. In *Religion of the Central Luo*, published in 1971, he addresses the history of Luo communities in Uganda, defines the metaphysical nature of the supreme god Jok, and elaborates upon
the social function of ritual. He explains how the traditional religion unified
lineages and cemented loyalties among different chiefdoms. He maintains
that although belief in many of the Acholi deities was shaken by colonialism, the traditional religious system is tenacious and persistent and still functions as the glue which holds many communities together. Overall, his
religious theses correct western accounts of traditional religion and call for
reconstructed Afro-centered myths which will provide a foundation for the
new nations of Africa.

Throughout his life, p'Bitek also published essays on a wide variety of
topics ranging from literature to politics to popular music. *Africa's Cultural
Revolution*, published in 1973, collects essays written for East African news-
papers, magazines, and periodicals between 1964 and 1971. The essays consistently call for the replacement of foreign cultures with African culture. He
also underscores the responsibility of the writer to probe the deep roots of
truth by teasing and pricking the conscience of society. Other essays collected in *Artist, the Ruler: Essays on Art, Culture, and Values*, published in 1986,
elaborate these themes. In this work, p'Bitek claims that every human being
is an artist and each individual is responsible for building a new Africa.

Resources

ATKINSON, RONALD. *The Roots of Ethnicity: The Origins of the Acholi of Uganda before
     1800*. Philadelphia: University of Pennsylvania Press, 1994. A study of the ori-
     gin and history of the Acholi people with bibliographic sources.
AYODO, AWUOR. "Definitions of the Self in Luo Women's Orature." *Research in
     African Literatures* 25, 3 (Fall 1994): 121–129. Review of women portrayed in
     other oral literature in East Africa.
BODUNDE, CHARLES A. "Oral Traditions and Modern Poetry: Okot p'Bitek's *Song of
     Lawino* and Okigbo's *Labyrinths*." In E. D. Jones, ed., *Orature in African Literature
     Today*, 24–34. Trenton, N.J.: Africa World Press, 1992. A brief discussion of the
     symbols used in *Song of Lawino*.

COOK, DAVID, and DAVID RUBADIRI, eds. *Poems from East Africa*. Portsmouth, N.H.: Heinemann, 1992. A collection of poems including Okot p'Bitek's "Return the Bridewealth" and "They Sowed and Watered."

DUERDEN, DENNIS, ed. "Okot p'Bitek." In *African Writers Talking*, 149–155. New York: Africana Publishing Company, 1972. Robert Serumaga's interview with p'Bitek in London, February, 1967.

GIRLING, F. K. *The Acholi of Uganda*. London: H.M. Stationery Office, 1960. Background information on the Acholi people.

HERON, G. A. *The Poetry of Okot p'Bitek*. London: Heinemann, 1976. A careful study of p'Bitek's work with focus on his characterization and satirical techniques.

————. "Introduction." In Okot p'Bitek, *Song of Lawino, Song of Ocol*, 1–33. Portsmouth, N.H.: Heinemann, 1984. An excellent review of p'Bitek's life and work.

KERR, DAVID. *African Popular Theatre*. Portsmouth, N.H.: Heinemann, 1995. An insightful discussion of theatre in Africa with reference to p'Bitek and Ngugi.

KNAPPERT, JAN. *The A–Z of African Proverbs*. London: Karnak House, 1989. A collection of African proverbs on a variety of themes.

LINDFORDS, BERNTH. "The Songs of Okot p'Bitek." In *Popular Literature in Africa*, 61–77. Trenton, N.J.: Africa World Press, 1991. A brief review of p'Bitek's life and work.

LO LIYONG, TABAN. *Eating Chiefs*. London: Heinemann, 1970. A collection of oral literature representing Luo culture including many Acholi stories.

————. "On Translating the 'Untranslated': Chapter 14 of *Wer pa Lawino* by Okot p'Bitek." *Research in African Literatures* 24, 3 (Fall 1993): 87–92. An English translation of the last chapter of *Song of Lawino*, which was not included in the English version of the poem by p'Bitek.

MAJA-PEARCE, ADEWALE, ed. *The Heinemann Book of African Poetry in English*. Portsmouth, N.H.: Heinemann, 1990. A collection of poetry by artists representing a variety of African countries.

NGARA, EMMANUEL. "Cultural Nationalism and Form in Okot p'Bitek." In *Ideology and Form in African Poetry*, 60–76. Portsmouth, N.H.: Heinemann, 1990. A discussion of p'Bitek's four songs.

OFCANSKY, THOMAS. *Uganda: Tarnished Pearl of Africa*. Boulder, Col.: Westview Press, 1995. A review of the history, society, and culture of Uganda.

OFUANI, OGO. "Old Wine in New Skins? An Exploratory Review of Okot p'Bitek's *White Teeth: A Novel*." *Research in African Literatures* 27, 2 (Summer 1996): 185–193. A review of the novel and a discussion of the difficulties involved in translation.

————. "The Poet as Self-Critic: Repercussions of Textual Revisions in Okot p'Bitek's *Song of Ocol*." *Research in African Literatures* 25, 4 (Winter 1994): 159–176. A discussion of p'Bitek's three texts of *Song of Ocol*.

OKPEWHO, ISIDORE. *African Oral Literature: Backgrounds, Character, and Continuity*. Bloomington: Indiana University Press, 1992. A detailed study of oral literature including background, types, themes, and adaptations.

OKUMU, CHARLES. "The Form of Okot p'Bitek's Poetry: Literary Borrowing from Acoli Oral Traditions." *Research in African Literatures* 23, 3 (Fall 1992): 54–66. A discussion of how the humor, satire, and lament of Lawino reflect Acoli poetic forms.

RUBADIRI, DAVID. "The Development of Writing in East Africa." In Christopher Heywood, ed., *Perspectives on African Literature*. London: Heinemann, 1979. A discussion of p'Bitek's influence on writing in East Africa.

SCHEUB, HAROLD. *The African Storyteller: Stories from African Oral Traditions.* Dubuque, Iowa: Kendall/Hunt Publishing Co., 1990. A collection of stories about gods, tricksters, heroes, and heroines from a wide variety of African ethnic groups.

SENANU, K. D., and T. VINCENT, eds. *A Selection of African Poetry.* London: Longman, 1988. A collection of poetry including p'Bitek's *Song of Malaya.*

A Selected Bibliography of Okot p'Bitek's Work

"Oral Literature and Its Social Background among the Acholi and Lang'o." B.Litt. Thesis, University of Oxford, 1964.

Song of Lawino. Nairobi: East Africa Publishing House, 1966; Cleveland: World Meridian Books, 1969. Published with *Song of Ocol*, Portsmouth, N.H.: Heinemann, 1984.

Song of Ocol. Nairobi: East Africa Publishing House, 1970. Published with *Song of Lawino*, Portsmouth, N.H.: Heinemann, 1984.

African Religions in Western Scholarship. Nairobi: East African Literature Bureau, 1970; Totowa, N.J.: Rowman and Littlefield, 1972.

Religion of the Central Luo. Nairobi: East African Literature Bureau, 1971.

Song of Prisoner. New York: The Third Press, Joseph Okpaku Publishing Co., 1971.

Two Songs (Song of Malaya and Song of Prisoner). Nairobi: East Africa Publishing House, 1971; Nairobi: Heinemann, 1988.

Africa's Cultural Revolution. Nairobi: Macmillan, 1973.

Horn of My Love. London: Heinemann, 1974; New York: Humanities Press, 1974.

Artist, the Ruler: Essays on Art, Culture, and Values. Nairobi: Heinemann, 1986.

Lak Tar. White Teeth. (Originally published in 1953 as *Lak Tar Miyo Kinyero Wi Lobo*, or *Are Your Teeth White? Then Laugh!*) Nairobi: Heinemann, 1989.

KENYA

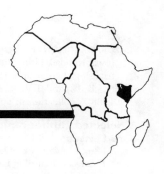

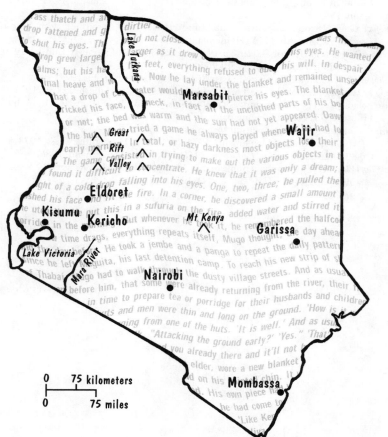

NGUGI WA THIONG'O CHRONICLES THE HISTORY OF THE GIKUYU
PEOPLE, WHO ORIGINALLY INHABITED THE AREAS SOUTH AND WEST OF
MOUNT KENYA.

Chapter 4

▼▼▼▼▼▼▼▼▼▼▼

Ngugi wa Thiong'o and
A Grain of Wheat

Writing in Kikuyu, Swahili, and English, Ngugi wa Thiong'o is the most prolific contemporary writer in East Africa. His first three novels form a trilogy which chronicles the history of the Gikuyu people. The Gikuyu creation myth is introduced, juxtaposed to the arrival of the British in *The River Between*; the Mau Mau opposition to British colonial forces is illustrated in *Weep Not Child*; and the birth of independent Kenya is celebrated in *A Grain of Wheat*. The complex psychological novel *A Grain of Wheat*, published in 1967, presents the freedom struggle as part of the great cycle of life. The main issue raised by the novel is independence—a concept which is viewed through the prism of the courage, mixed loyalties, treachery, and redemption of five freedom fighters: Kihika, Mugo, Gikonyo, Mumbi, and Karanja. The psychological complexities of the characters are explored in terms of personal catharsis involving commitment, betrayal, and reconciliation. This movement refers to the birth of independent Kenya and tentatively heralds the dawn of a new age. *A Grain of Wheat* is appropriate for students on the upper or advanced levels in history, literature, or psychology courses. The first two novels in the trilogy are appropriate for students on the lower and intermediate levels.

A Grain of Wheat and the Gikuyu People of Kenya
A Grain of Wheat is a powerful historical novel which focuses on national and personal revolution in Kenya. The setting is the area surrounding the village of Thabai, and the present action of the novel takes place immediately before and after the Independence Day ceremonies held on December 12, 1963. However, the story recounts the history of the Gikuyu people and the struggle of the Mau Mau freedom fighters through a series of flashbacks, recollections, and interior monologues.

The first major flashback reviews the creation myth of Gikuyu and Mumbi, the first parents of the Gikuyu people to whom Ngai, the supreme god, gave the land surrounding Mount Kenya. The flashback also reviews the prophecy of Mugo wa Kibiro, a prophet in the nineteenth century who predicted the coming of the white man. The seed or a grain of wheat identified in the flashback refers to Waiyaki, a freedom fighter who had been buried alive with his head thrust into the center of the earth. Waiyaki was like a seed that gave birth to the Mau Mau freedom movement. A second grain of wheat is introduced in Kihika, the deceased freedom fighter who was known as the burning spear of the land and the terror of the British colonists. It was Kihika who intensified the emergency in the 1950s by killing District Officer Robson. He was betrayed by his own people, viciously tortured by white settlers, and finally hanged at Rung'ei Market.

The novel frames the Mau Mau freedom movement in terms of history and religious tradition. The Gikuyu believed in their god-given land rights and the never-ending cycle of life. According to the ancient creation myth, when Ngai, the supreme creator god, divided the universe, he gave a man named Gikuyu the panorama of land in East Africa viewed from the summit of Mount Kenya. Ngai then commanded Gikuyu to establish a homestead and gave him a beautiful wife named Mumbi, whose name means "the molder of children." Gikuyu and Mumbi loved one another deeply and gave birth to nine daughters who founded the principal clans of the Gikuyu nation.

Historically, the Gikuyu developed an agrarian economy based on grains, yams, sugarcane, and bananas; land was crucial and the concept of private property owned by a family was the traditional basis of land tenure. Traditionally, every section of land had its owner and fixed boundary, and the overall territory made up a unified nation which the Gikuyu defended collectively.

However, in the 1880s an astonishing prophecy revealed the tragic fate of the Gikuyu land. The revered diviner Mugo wa Kibiro, emerging from a nightmarish experience mute, shaken, and covered with bruises, predicted the arrival of strangers with skins like pale frogs and clothes like butterflies carrying magical fire-spitting sticks. Mogo indicated that a huge, indestructible iron snake resembling a centipede would follow the pale skins. Sadly, he prophesied that the land would be appropriated by the strangers, and the Gikuyu would be powerless against the foreign, land-eating force of the white settlers and their railroads.

As the seer predicted, the British arrived, colonized, and finally claimed Kenya in the "Scramble for Africa." The early missionaries, who had set up the first mission station in Mombassa in 1846, were followed by others, including the explorer David Livingstone. Likewise, the early traders involved in the Ugandan caravan routes were followed by the Imperial British East Africa Company, a private company chartered to develop commerce in East Africa in 1888. Britain claimed Kenya as a protectorate in 1895 and annexed most of present-day Kenya as a colony in 1920.

A Grain of Wheat reflects the Gikuyu people's response to the changes introduced by the British colonists as the plot dramatizes the end of the Mau Mau rebellion and a local celebration of Kenya's independence. There are actually five main characters in the novel, one dead and four living: Kihika, Mumbi, Gikonyo, Karanja, and Mugo. Kihika is a deceased Mau Mau freedom fighter who is like a "living-dead," who lives on in the memory of his comrades. His life and death give courage to the other main characters. The four living characters are defined in relationship to Kihika and in relationship to one another. Kihika's sister Mumbi also supports the Mau Mau freedom struggle. Gikonyo is married to Mumbi; he fought beside Kihika in the struggle for freedom, and he has also served six years in political detention for his work with the Mau Mau. Because Karanja served as a homeguard loyal to the settlers, he has been the major suspect accused of betraying Kihika to the British. Mugo, whose name means "man of God" in the Kikuyu language, was encouraged by Kihika to join the Mau Mau movement when in fact he only wished to remain isolated and uncommitted.

As past events are woven into their life stories, each character moves through the cycle of life. First, by virtue of being a Gikuyu at this point in history, each character is born into the struggle for independence. Every character except Karanja experiences growth, and each one seems to make a commitment, thereby moving from childhood to maturity. The beautiful Mumbi commits herself to her husband, Gikonyo; Gikonyo commits himself to the Mau Mau movement; and Karanja commits himself to the colonial status quo. The disgruntled Mugo's commitment to the freedom struggle is questionable.

Each character also experiences a type of symbolic death through guilt and betrayal. At a point of hysterical relief, Mumbi succumbs to the sexual advances of her husband's rival, Karanja; in his desire to return to his family, Gikonyo confesses that he has taken the Mau Mau oath; and as a newly appointed colonial chief, Karanja sells the secrets of the Mau Mau revolution to the British. Although undisclosed at first, Mugo's lengthy symbolic death-in-life experience is caused by the fact that he is the real traitor of the freedom fighter Kihika.

After these experiences of betrayal, all of the characters, with the exception of Karanja, experience rebirth through reconciliation. Mugo is the first to move from spiritual death to life. Through his private confession to

Mumbi and his public proclamation to the crowd gathered at the Independence Day celebrations, Mugo admits that he betrayed Kihika, and thereby liberates himself and others from the death-grip of guilt. In his climactic speech, Mugo identifies himself as the Judas who sold Kihika to the white man and led him to his death. Therefore, it seems as if the independence celebrations in Rung'ei, the very place where Kihika was hanged, have become a ceremony for a traitor. Likewise, Kenyan independence may be nothing more than a celebration of the profound betrayal of the Gikuyu people by the neocolonial elite. Nevertheless, Mugo's symbolic death is yet another grain of wheat symbolizing a spiritual rebirth, for his confession liberates others.

Mugo's reconciliation with the truth is paralleled with the recognition of guilt and the rebirth of Mumbi and Gikonyo's love. New life grows out of forgiveness and the promise of reunion. At the end of the novel, Mumbi seems open to forgiving Gikonyo's hard-hearted attitude toward her, and Gikonyo seems to forgive Mumbi for her liaison with Karanja. He begins to accept the child she conceived with his rival and plans a new life as he imagines the wedding stool he will carve for her from the Muiri wood of Mount Kenya. This symbol of peace and reconciliation will feature a thin man with hard lines on his face reaching out to a woman; together they will be intertwined with a third figure—a child. Other symbols will tell the story: a field stands in need of cultivation, a hoe symbolizes the hard work necessary to cultivate the field, and a bean flower represents fertility. As the novel closes, Gikonyo dreams of carving a woman big with child on the wedding stool. He hopes that his renewed love and union with Mumbi will result in new life.

A Grain of Wheat illustrates the Gikuyu people's response to the British colonists who streamed into Kenya and settled in the areas owned by the Gikuyu. These settlers drove away the individual Gikuyu landowners and developed huge farms and ranches that produced coffee, tea, wheat, cattle, and dairy products. The British called the Gikuyu lands the "white highlands," and as the colonists developed their estates, the majority of the Gikuyu people were confined to "tribal reserves."

Loss of the land destroyed life for the Gikuyu. Traditional agricultural techniques required large tracts of land, allowing certain plots to remain fallow each year, and the soil of the restricted reserve was soon exhausted by continuous planting. As the population increased, the agriculturally based economy declined, and the Gikuyu people sank into poverty. Consequently, Gikuyu men were forced to migrate to the European community of Nairobi in search of employment. These workers were subjected to a degrading system of registration known as *kipande* and were forced to carry pass-like identification. Initially, Gikuyu men were hired as household servants and laborers on the settlers' plantations. In some cases, the Gikuyu men cultivated the very lands owned by their fathers and forefathers. As industry developed, Gikuyu men also served as a cheap labor force in the factories. The urban migration separated the men from their families and destroyed many aspects of traditional life in the Gikuyu villages.

The European settlers failed to understand that Gikuyu society was truly rooted in the soil and turned deaf ears on Gikuyu demands for the redistribution of their ancestral lands. Instead, the British government conscripted thousands of Gikuyu men to fight in World War II, which ironically provided the impetus for Kenyan land rights and the independence struggle. After the war, British Kenya failed to reward her Kenyan soldiers, called for more European settlers, and offered Gikuyu land to European ex-servicemen. The landless, disenfranchised Gikuyu ex-servicemen were stunned and opted to work for freedom through the militant action known as the Mau Mau rebellion rather than settle for a life of poverty and servitude.

The Mau Mau freedom struggle was a grassroots movement that created great division among the people of Kenya. In 1946 a Gikuyu nationalist leader named Jomo Kenyatta returned from Europe and founded the Kenyan African Union. Within this constituency, leaders of various ethnic groups throughout Kenya discussed the need for unity, but unrest grew as Mau Mau freedom fighters implemented a guerrilla campaign in the forests surrounding traditional Gikuyu territory. The Mau Mau movement culminated in 1952 when the British government declared a state of emergency and arrested Kenyatta as the genius of the insurrection. The Kenyan African Union was banned, and after a questionable trial, Kenyatta was sentenced to eight years in prison.

The Mau Mau rebellion, as it was called by the British, consisted of young Gikuyu men and women who risked their lives in an armed struggle in the forests and mountains north of Nairobi. The freedom fighters were supported by thousands of Gikuyu people in the "homelands" and other Africans throughout Kenya. It is estimated that over 15,000 Mau Mau freedom fighters and African troops loyal to the British were killed in fierce fighting during the freedom struggle. In contrast, the total casualties for European Kenyans was minimal.

Tragically, throughout the struggle, the British colonial government publicized the Mau Mau as terrorists. Neither the colonial government nor Britain herself ever acknowledged that the Mau Mau movement was a military revolution seeking freedom and the restoration of Gikuyu land. Many modern Kenyans still believe that the Mau Mau revolution is a shadowy period that should be buried and forgotten; others regard the freedom struggle as a spiritual and historical turning point for Kenya.

Literary Techniques in **A Grain of Wheat**

The present action of the novel covers five days leading up to *Uhuru*, the Independence Day celebrations on December 12, 1963, and several days thereafter. Nevertheless, seventy years of history are presented through a series of flashbacks and recollections; furthermore, interior monologues, dreams, visions, and a stream-of-consciousness discourse heighten the internal struggle of individual characters. These techniques link the past with the present as various incidents and places cause characters to remember the freedom struggle.

The first three chapters set the scene. In the first chapter, Mugo and the concepts of *uhuru* (freedom) and *kazi* (work) are introduced on the eve of independence. Chapter Two lays out the Gikuyu creation myth and provides historical background reminding the reader of the pioneer freedom fighters and the sacrifices of the Mau Mau. Kihika is introduced as a second grain of wheat, following Waiyaki, who has died to bring new life and redemption to the people of Kenya. The third chapter returns to the present, and Mugo is asked to lead the Independence Day celebrations and honor Kihika as Kenya's Moses.

Throughout the rest of the novel, a portrait of life in colonial Kenya and the story of each major character emerges as the layers of narrative move from present to past and back to present. For example, Mugo's fear of involvement, unwillingness to take the Mau Mau oath, and betrayal of Kihika are exposed through recollections and flashbacks. Interior monologues, dreams, and visions reveal Mugo's internal strife as he is tormented by guilt. Flashbacks also identify Karanja as the prime suspect in Kihika's murder and define him as the homeguard chief who chooses to serve the whites in order to save himself. Mumbi and Gikonyo's story is also told through a series of flashbacks, for the reader learns about the race in which Gikonyo won Mumbi's love, his dedication to the Mau Mau, and his six years in political detention. Gikonyo recalls his burning desire to be reunited with Mumbi as the hope that sustained him throughout the struggle, and Mumbi's recollections reveal her suffering during the emergency. Overall, Ngugi uses a variety of literary techniques to create layers of the past throughout the novel. He thereby implies that the future will naturally unfold from the present as the present has evolved from the past.

Points to Ponder

The question of Mugo's character is a crucial issue for students to explore. Does Mugo truly wish to live in isolation from his community, or is he a pathetic, tragic figure struggling with internal conflicts that have turned him into an anti-hero? Why didn't Mugo take the oath of baptism into the Mau

Mau freedom struggle, and why did he hate Kihika so viciously? Is Mugo's betrayal of Kihika an act of moral courage or an act of selfish cowardice? Does Mugo move from death to life through his relationship with the deceased Kihika? Furthermore, how do the other main characters, Mumbi, Gikonyo, and Karanja, relate to Kihika? How do these characters move through the cycle of life from birth to growth to death and rebirth in the freedom struggle? Minor characters add a variety of dimensions to the freedom struggle including Gitogo, the deaf-mute; Githua, the legless hero; and General R. What role do these characters play?

Other issues concern the overarching themes of revolution and independence in the novel. In what ways does the theme of personal revolution echo the Gikuyu nation's revolution through the Mau Mau freedom struggle? Are the characters in the novel who move through the death experience to rebirth similar to the Gikuyu people who move from oppression to freedom? In what way does the birth of the new independent Kenya parallel the growth of individual freedom fighters who achieve new life through reconciliation and love?

The portrayal of women and the relationships of women to one another are also important issues in the novel. How does Mumbi reflect the first woman of the Gikuyu creation myth, and why is she named for this ancestor? How does Mumbi's experience of the freedom struggle on the home front compare with Wambui's experience carrying Mau Mau secrets from the villages into the forest with a pistol tied to her thighs? How does Mumbi compare with other women in the novel such as Wangari, Njeri, and Wambuku? Why are the men in the novel so attracted to Mumbi?

The title of the novel echoes I Corinthians 15:36 which teaches that the seed a farmer sows is not quickened to life unless it dies. What is the significance of the title of the novel? What does the grain of wheat symbolize? Is the author suggesting that the future will grow from the present, and true social revolution will bring new life to Kenya? Must the political will and the desire for freedom die in order to be reborn? What will freedom from colonial rule mean to the Gikuyu people? Does freedom depend on the recognition of guilt and the power of reconciliation, love, and hard work? How do the reunited lovers Gikonyo and Mumbi echo the union of the first parents and symbolize the potential rebirth of Kenyan society as a whole?

Finally, the scene which Gikonyo carves on his stool is reminiscent of the traditional tree of life which celebrates the interrelationship of all members of the family including the beautiful ones who are yet unborn. In traditional Gikuyu religion, this concept is augmented by the cycle of life—a cycle through which an individual passes through the basic phases of birth, life, death, and new life. A more in-depth understanding of the cycle of life within the traditional religious world view may be helpful in addressing many of the issues raised by *A Grain of Wheat* and analyzing how the characters move through death to new life.

The Cycle of Life in the Traditional Gikuyu World View

According to the Gikuyu world view, the cycle of life is rooted in the community which is rooted in the Earth. Land is crucial, and the Earth is the most sacred entity in life. Mother Earth nurtures and sustains her people, and her soil feeds every child throughout his or her cycle of life on earth. Therefore, the Gikuyu people swear by the soil in an everlasting, unbreakable oath, for even after life, the soil nurtures the spirits of the dead and buried. The earth also symbolizes a link of communication between the living and the dead.

Gikuyu society is based entirely on an age-grade system whereby an individual moves through clearly defined phases of life related to the living and the dead. The life stages educate the individual and define status, privilege, and responsibility. The major phases of life are marked by ritual sacrifices and prayers, most of which involve communication with the ancestors.

A child enters life at birth; at that time a name is given which often reflects the child's relationship to the ancestors. After birth, the father places a small bracelet of goatskin on the child signifying that he or she is a full person in the Gikuyu society. Then, when the child is old enough to herd goats, another rite features bracelets which symbolize the bond between the child and the entire nation. These bracelets represent a link in the long chain of life, connecting the child with both the living and the departed. The ring symbolizes the life cycle, which links the generations of the long distant past with the generations of the present. At an early age, the child learns that this sacred link must never be broken. Later, when he or she can reason and remember, a child reenacts his or her physical birth by being placed between his or her mother's legs. The child is bound to the mother with a goat's intestine. This symbolic second birth, which is performed before initiation, signifies that the child has been born again, and is prepared to continue moving through the cycle of life.

Initiation is the next crucial phase in the life cycle and marks the passage of an individual from childhood into adulthood. This rite, which includes the surgical circumcision of boys and girls, is accompanied by preparation, education, ritual dances, songs, and a period of healing. After initiation, the young adult is considered a fully mature Gikuyu who knows right from wrong and who is responsible enough to marry, found a homestead, bury his parents, inherit property, and take part in certain rituals. Initiation is an absolutely essential link in Gikuyu life through which the individual is born into adulthood.

Adulthood is marked by marriage, which bestows superior status on an individual. After the first child is born, parents are initiated into the company of elders and allowed to take part in ritual ceremonies. Eventually, an individual will become an elder of the *Kiama*, or the "Gikuyu Court of Elders," and thereby entitled to administer law and justice. The elders are revered, for they will soon journey through death and join the ancestors.

Death is a threshold into the next stage of Gikuyu life—life after death. The departed who are still remembered by the living are often known as the "living-dead," or ancestors who have left the material world but who have achieved a state of immortality by living on in the memory and daily life of the living. These ancestors are remembered not only through the names of their descendants, but also through songs, stories, dances, and rituals. The living-dead are still considered people by the Gikuyu and return to their human families periodically to give advice concerning ethical matters, family activities, and traditions. Basically, the ancestors act as intermediaries between God and humankind, and the ritual remembrance of the ancestors is celebrated in a variety of crucial ceremonies. Only when the living-dead pass on into the dark and shadowy world of the forgotten do they become the dead-dead. At this point, the soul of the individual ceases to live on. Therefore, elders who are approaching the threshold of death impress the importance of remembering the ancestors upon young Gikuyu. These elders have a vested interest in training the youth to remember their ancestors well.

The traditional cycle of Gikuyu life presents life after death as remembrance rather than resurrection, for the relationship between the living and the living-dead is one of reverent remembrance, communication, and communion. Although the ancestors are honored, prayer and worship are reserved only for Ngai, the almighty creator god, whose movement is signaled by thunder and lightning as he travels from one sacred place to another.

The Author and His Work

Ngugi wa Thiong'o

The son of a Gikuyu farmer, Ngugi wa Thiong'o was born in Kamiriithu, Limuru in 1938. As a young boy, he studied at Kamaandura Mission School and Maanguu, one of the Gikuyu independent schools, before enrolling in Alliance High School. He then attended Makerere University in Uganda, where he studied English literature, concentrating on the work of D. H. Lawrence and Joseph Conrad. As a student, Ngugi wrote his first play in 1962 entitled *The Black Hermit*, which was produced for the Uganda National Theatre as part of the nation's independence celebrations. He also wrote his first two novels, *The River Between* and *Weep Not Child*, while he was an undergraduate. Appearing in 1964, *Weep Not Child* was the first novel published by an East African writer in English and won awards from the East African Literature Bureau and the Dakar Festival of Negro Arts. Although *The River Between* was published a year later in 1965, this novel was actually written first and provides the basis for *Weep Not Child*. As a young writer, Ngugi published under his Christian name, James Ngugi.

After graduation from Makerere University, Ngugi worked on Nairobi's *Daily Nation* for a short time and then went on to graduate school at the University of Leeds. Here he discovered the work of Karl Marx and Frantz Fanon, and composed his third novel, *A Grain of Wheat*, which was published in 1967. Upon returning to Kenya, Ngugi took a position as a special lecturer in English at Nairobi's University College. He abandoned the Christian name James for his traditional Gikuyu name, and became the editor of *Zuka: A Journal of East African Creative Writing*. In 1969 the student body went on strike and the college closed; Ngugi resigned in protest of the severe measures taken by the administration against the students and left Kenya to teach for one year at the University of Illinois. He continued writing and published a collection of three plays entitled *This Time Tomorrow*, as well as a variety of essays in magazines such as *The New African* and *Zuka*.

In 1972, Ngugi was appointed head of the Department of Literature at the University of Nairobi where he sought to replace the study of English literature and culture with the study of African literature and culture. During this time, he collected some of his essays on African and Caribbean literature in a volume entitled *Homecoming*, which was published in 1972. He also published a collection of short stories entitled *Secret Lives* in 1975, and a novel entitled *Petals of Blood* in 1977.

Ngugi continued his work as a dramatist, and in 1976 co-authored a play with Micere Githae Mugo entitled *The Trial of Dedan Kimathi*. This work portrayed the tragedy of an heroic leader of the Mau Mau resistance and was presented at Festac '77 in Lagos. The drama was also presented at the Kenyan National Theatre in Nairobi during the "Kenyatta Day" celebrations; however, the government authorities canceled the play after a few performances. Many Kenyans, including Ngugi, were enraged that the authorities did not allow the play to run throughout the month celebrating the victory of the Mau Mau freedom fighters.

Undaunted however, Ngugi continued writing and faced the greatest turning point in his life later in 1977 when he co-authored a play with Ngugi wa Mirii in the Kikuyu language entitled *Ngaahika Ndeenda*, or *I Will Marry When I Want*. The play featured local peasants and workers as actors and was produced by local Gikuyu people in a theatre built by the Kamiriithu community. However, this production was also short-lived, for the government deemed it provocative and subversive. Ngugi was detained in the maximum security prison of Kamiti for approximately one year; no charges were levied against the author, however, and he was never brought to trial. Three years later in 1980, the play was published in Kikuyu by Heinemann and went into three printings in three months. The overwhelming popular response to *I Will Marry When I Want* convinced Ngugi of the importance of writing in a language Kenyan citizens could understand.

During his incarceration, Ngugi wrote his prison memoirs and published *Detained: A Writer's Prison Diary* in 1981. He also started writing a novel in Kikuyu on carefully hidden sheets of toilet paper. The manuscript was discovered and confiscated by prison guards; it was not destroyed, however, but eventually returned to the author. The novel was published as *Caitaani Mutharaba-ini* in Kikuyu in 1980 and as *Devil on the Cross* in English in 1982. The powerful oral reading of the novel in Kikuyu in neighborhood bars echoed the oral literature of the past and resulted in a surprising revelation to both the people and the author. The Kenyan people realized that true freedom had never been won, and Ngugi realized that the fighting peasantry could not read any of the work he published in English.

A volume of essays entitled *Writers in Politics* addressing the relevance of literature to life was published in 1981, and in 1982 Ngugi left Kenya to continue his writing and teaching in the United States. The novel *Matigari* was written and published in Kikuyu in 1986 and translated into English in 1987. In 1993, Ngugi published another collection of essays entitled *Moving the Centre: The Struggle for Cultural Freedoms* which challenged artists to seek freedom from western cultural dominance.

Currently, Ngugi wa Thiong'o serves as Professor of Comparative Literature and Performance Studies at New York University, and an international conference focusing on his work titled "Ngugi wa Thiong'o Texts and Contexts" was hosted by Pennsylvania State University in 1994. Ngugi wa Thiong'o continues to write and has developed an interest in children's books and film. He lives in self-exile in the United States while maintaining his interest in the plight of the Kenyan people.

Ngugi wa Thiong'o's Work

Ngugi wa Thiong'o has dedicated his art to the freedom struggle. In addition to illustrating historical themes, he calls for social justice, addresses the crucial issue of language and African literature, and challenges other writers to reconsider writing in indigenous languages. His early novels document the effects of colonialism on the Gikuyu people, the plight of the landless peasantry in colonial Kenya, and the complex struggles of the Mau Mau freedom fighters. The themes are based upon the fundamental rights of the Gikuyu people to retain their God-given land and reclaim tracts appropriated by the British during the colonial era. However, Ngugi's later novels satirize the neocolonial elite who imitate their former oppressors and create a new world of corruption and oppression in modern Kenya. In addition, in his critical work, Ngugi charges artists with the power and responsibility of decolonizing the minds of the oppressed and challenges writers to become creative centers of energy for the poor by striving for cultural freedom.

Ngugi's first three novels form a trilogy which chronicles the history of the Gikuyu people. The first novel in this trilogy was originally titled *The Black Messiah* and was published in 1965 as *The River Between*. The novel sets out the conceptual and religious framework of the Gikuyu people in the fundamental Gikuyu creation myth, which recounts God's giving of the land surrounding Mount Kenya to Gikuyu and Mumbi. This myth is not only the cornerstone of the traditional Gikuyu world view, but it sets the historical backdrop for the infiltration and influence of European settlers who introduce the complex issues of Christianity and formal western education in East Africa. The protagonist, Waiyaki, is a young optimistic teacher. He is charged by his father, the seer, to honor traditional Gikuyu values as he learns the new, unfamiliar wisdom of the white settlers. As Waiyaki pursues his goal, two disparate communities of Gikuyu people emerge: the Christian Gikuyu community and the traditional Gikuyu community, who are divided over the issues of religion and education. Waiyaki believes that education is the key to progress—the secret that will allow the Gikuyu people to live in peace with one another and benefit from the changes introduced by the white settlers. However, in his zealous pursuit of education for all, Waiyaki fails to recognize that reconciliation must form the foundation of unity within the Gikuyu people. He therefore fails to straddle the divide between the Christianized and traditional Gikuyu factions and is unable to lead his people through the turbulent colonial times.

The second novel of the trilogy is entitled *Weep Not Child*. This novel was actually published first, in 1964, and won great international acclaim. Here Ngugi continues to chronicle the history of the Gikuyu people during the colonial period just prior to the Mau Mau revolution. The story focuses on a young boy named Njoroge and his family. Ngotho, Njoroge's father, symbolizes the landless peasantry who have been stripped of their ancestral lands by the colonial settlers. Ngotho tenderly cares for the plants on his white employer's farm and loves the land, for it is the land of his forefathers, the land given to the Gikuyu people by God. Njoroge's entire family suffers from the injustices of colonial rule—particularly Boro, Njoroge's brother, who is broken and bitter after serving the British in World War II. As Boro joins the freedom struggle of the Mau Mau, his family suffers the revenge of the British government. As he experiences the devastating effects of the Mau Mau revolution, young Njoroge passes from childhood into adulthood and finally emerges as a tentative young adult who chooses freedom and life over oppression and death.

Ngugi published extensively over the next five years. Appearing in 1967, *A Grain of Wheat* completes the trilogy and stands as Ngugi's masterpiece celebrating the independence of modern Kenya from Britain. This work was followed by a play published in 1968 entitled *The Black Hermit*, which tells the story of Remi, a young man who is dubbed the black hermit because he chooses to leave the village of his youth to attend university in the city. *This Time Tomorrow*, a collection of three plays, was published in 1970 and depicts how colonialism rent asunder the fabric of traditional life. In 1975, Ngugi also published a collection of short stories entitled *Secret Lives*, which focuses on the tragedies affecting women, the problems created by the Europeans, and the loneliness of city life in post-independent Kenya. In the same year, Ngugi published *Homecoming: Essays on African and Caribbean Literature, Culture, and Politics*, a collection which examines key issues concerning culture and the writer's responsibility to maintain cultural integrity. In this volume, Ngugi also reviews the works of Chinua Achebe and Okot p'Bitek and explores ways in which African people can maintain their cultural heritage.

In 1976, *The Trial of Dedan Kimathi*, which Ngugi co-authored with a Gikuyu woman named Micere Githae Mugo, elicited a tremendous emotional response from Kenyan audiences. Written to commemorate the Mau Mau leaders who initiated the freedom struggle, the play depicts the trial of one of the revolution's most popular heroes—Dedan Kimathi. Kimathi served as a field marshal during the Mau Mau freedom struggle; he was later brought to trial and hung by the British. The historical drama seeks to locate the freedom struggle in generations of rebellion dating back to the fifteenth century when the people of East Africa attempted to resist the Portuguese. The hero not only defies imperialism, but all the powers of the industrialized world. His death at the hands of the colonial masters makes him a martyr for the oppressed.

Ngugi's bitterness about the intervention of the Ministry of Social

Services and the limited productions of *The Trial of Dedan Kimathi* in the National Theatre in Nairobi fueled his mounting discontent with the neocolonial government and fired his later work. *Petals of Blood, I Will Marry When I Want, Detained, Devil on the Cross,* and *Matigari* all reflect Ngugi's growing cynicism and disgust with the neocolonial regime in modern Kenya.

Petals of Blood was published in 1977 and portrays a decrepit and deteriorated Kenya after a decade of independent rule. The essential elements of Kenyan life have been destroyed by the self-interest of Kenya's corrupt businessmen and politicians. In this complex novel, three prominent and corrupt leaders are burned to death in a brothel in the village of Ilmorog, and four characters, whose lives are intertwined, are arrested as suspects. Munira, Karega, Abdulla, and Wanja have all been disappointed by the neocolonial regime. All four have good reasons for seeking revenge on the three dead men, for the people of Ilmorog have not profited from the new enterprises they have created. As the townspeople unsuccessfully beg for help from their elected representatives, they travel back through their national conscience and painfully relive the suffering of the freedom struggle. Ngugi implies that the blood of the freedom fighters was shed in vain, for tragically, the impoverished, drought-stricken people of Ilmorog merit no share in the nation's resources.

In 1977 Ngugi founded the Kamiriithu Educational, Cultural, and Community Center. Here the famous drama he co-authored with Ngugi wa Mirii titled *Ngaahika Ndeenda* (or *I Will Marry When I Want*) was produced in Kikuyu by the local community. The drama featured actors and actresses selected from among the local peasants and workers and was produced in a theatre built by the Kamiriithu community. However, after a single month's run, the license for the production was revoked by the authorities because the play was considered provocative and potentially subversive. The drama focuses on a young woman's decision to defy authority and marry when she wants. The chorus of villagers and the din of life that provides the backdrop for her decision thoroughly denounces the evils of life in modern Kenya. The Satans of poverty—crime and oppression—are denounced, and the people wonder what has happened to their land. The heroes of the past have not been revered, and the modern politicians are eager to sell out the entire country to capitalistic foreign powers. Modern-day leaders are taunted as the "grabbers" and "eaters" of all that the working people have produced, and as experienced exploiters and oppressors, they simply shut their eyes to the plight of the poor. At the same time Heinemann published *I Will Marry When I Want* in English in 1982, the Kenyan government destroyed the Kamiriithu Community Center.

Ngugi was detained in prison in 1977 although the government never brought charges against him nor allowed him to stand trial. Throughout his incarceration, he remained totally defiant, and his prison memoirs titled *Detained: A Writer's Prison Diary* were published in 1981. This work describes the humiliation, degradation, and hopelessness of life in the Kamiti maximum security prison and includes reflections on politics in modern Kenya. As in his other works, Ngugi holds up the poor and oppressed citizens of Kenya and expresses his resentment toward the neocolonial government.

During his detention, Ngugi surreptitiously drafted a novel that was published as *Caitaani Mutharaba-ini* in Kikuyu in 1980 and as *Devil on the Cross* in English in 1982. The powerful oral reading of the novel in Gikuyu neighborhood gatherings echoed the oral literature of the past, and demand for the original Kikuyu edition was so great that upon publication, the novel was immediately reprinted. In this novel, modern capitalist Kenya is portrayed as a grotesque and greedy monster. Greed has become the code of ethics that has replaced traditional Gikuyu and Christian values, and a den of thieves representing the elite suggest increasingly corrupt plots for maximizing their own wealth and exploiting the working poor. As the thieves speak at the Devil's Feast, they plan to suck the blood, sweat, and brains out of the Kenyan workers; furthermore, the energies and talents of the Kenyan people will be exported to industrialized foreign countries. As the capitalistic schemes escalate, they are increasingly linked to sexual exploitation. A young woman named Wariinga, who has lost her job because she refuses to have sexual intercourse with her employer and who has been evicted from her dilapidated home because she refuses to pay the exorbitant rent, witnesses the Devil's Feast because she is anxious to understand the extent of corruption in modern Kenya. The author clearly states that the evils of modern society are devils which must be nailed to the cross in this tragic and grotesque story of contemporary Kenya—a modern nation enslaved by the power of Satan's capitalism and corruption.

In *Writers in Politics*, a collection of speeches and articles written between 1970 and 1980 and published in 1981, Ngugi calls for African writers and critics to act as the intellectual backbone of the anti-imperialist struggle. This work focuses on the relevance of literature to life and explores the role of literature and education in the struggle to define and maintain a patriotic national culture. The author discusses the role of writers in politics and illustrates his abhorrence of political repression.

As a result of his personal and professional freedom struggle, Ngugi left Kenya in 1982. His voice was not to be silenced, however. In 1986, he published *Decolonizing the Mind: The Politics of Language in African Literature*, which he dedicated to all those who write in African languages and to all those who over the years have maintained the dignity of the literature, culture, philosophy, and other treasures carried by African languages. In this work, Ngugi discusses a universal language of struggle, analyzes the relationship between African languages and African literature, and redefines the language of African literature. Ngugi states that this book is his farewell to English as a vehicle for his writing. Instead he will write in Kikuyu and Swahili and hope that through translation he will be able to maintain a dialogue with all readers.

Matigari is Ngugi's latest novel, published in 1987. This work was written in Kikuyu and translated into English by Wangui wa Goro, a social critic, interpreter, and writer who has translated all Ngugi's children's books into English. *Matigari* recaptures the oral tradition of a person named Matigari who is on a quest to find Ndiiro, an old man who can cure sickness. The novel becomes an allegory about Matigari, an old freedom fighter who emerges from the forest to reclaim the lands of his fathers and the great houses built by the African proletariat. However, this freedom fighter's struggle is no longer with the colonists but rather with the neocolonial bourgeoisie and the abject poverty of his descendants, the Gikuyu people of modern Kenya. The experiences of the exploited masses become an allegory as Matigari's mythic life story recaptures the past, present, and potential future of Kenya's people. Because Matigari has been secluded in the forest, he is untainted by the neocolonial corruption of the state and retains a clarity of vision. He befriends the children who sleep in the junkyard and live by eating garbage from the dump. Their leader, Muriki, represents all the children born into a corrupt postcolonial world. As Muriki reclaims Matigari's weapons and escapes into the forest, one hopes that the new generation will be able to revolutionize society with more lasting success than the Mau Mau freedom fighters.

Finally, in 1993, Ngugi published *Moving the Centre: The Struggle for Cultural Freedoms*, a collection of essays that rejects four hundred years of world domination by western powers. Ngugi calls for the movement of the center of western cultural, political, and economic power in order to create a world freed from cultural bondage. Again, the artist's power and responsibility is emphasized as Ngugi challenges writers within each nation to move away from the boundaries of race, religion, gender, and class, and toward a creative center of energy among working people. As a giant of African literature, Ngugi seeks to move the center of energy from the West to multiple cultures throughout the world and lifts up the writer as a crucial worker in the struggle for true cultural freedom.

Resources

AMUTA, CHIDI. *The Theory of African Literature: Implications for Practical Criticism*. London: Zed Books, 1989. An analysis of Ngugi's anti-imperialist drama and *Petals of Blood*.

BJORNSON, RICHARD, ed. *The Language Question.* Special edition of *Research in African Literatures* 23, 1 (Spring 1992). A collection of articles analyzing the issue of language in African literature.

CANTALUPO, CHARLES, ed. *The World of Ngugi wa Thiong'o.* Trenton, N.J.: Africa World Press, 1995. A review of Ngugi's later work including two interviews with the author.

COOK, DAVID, and MICHAEL OKENIMKPE. *Ngugi wa Thiong'o: An Exploration of His Writings.* London: Heinemann, 1983. A basic review of Ngugi's career and creative work through *Devil on the Cross,* with sections on the short stories and plays.

DAVISON, JEAN, with the women of Mutira. *Voices from Mutira: Lives of Rural Gikuyu Women.* Boulder, Col.: Lynne Rienner Publishers, 1989. Life stories of seven Gikuyu women ranging from twenty-three to seventy-five years of age in the Kirinyaga District of Kenya.

DECKER, JAMES. "Mugo and the Silence of Oppression." In Charles Cantalupo, ed., *The World of Ngugi wa Thiong'o,* 45–57. Trenton, N.J.: Africa World Press, 1995. An analysis of Mugo's silence as a symbol of oppression and his voice as a window of redemption in the freedom struggle.

DUERDEN, DENNIS, and COSMO PIETERSE, eds. "Ngugi wa Thiong'o." In *African Writers Talking.* New York: Africana Publishing Company, 1972. An interview with Ngugi.

FUREDI, FRANK. *The Mau Mau War in Perspective.* London: James Currey, and Athens, Ohio: Ohio University Press, 1991. An historical analysis of the Gikuyu land issues, the emergence of the Mau Mau revolution, and the subsequent decolonization of Kenya.

GIKANDI, SIMON. "Ngugi's Conversion: Writing and the Politics of Language." In *Research in African Literatures* 23, 1 (Spring 1992): 131–144. An analysis of Ngugi's decision to write in Kikuyu instead of English.

———. "The Political Novel: Community, Character, and Consciousness in Sembene Ousmane's *God's Bits of Wood,* Alex La Guma's *In the Fog of the Season's End,* and Ngugi's *Petals of Blood.*" In *Reading the African Novel,* 111–148. London: Heinemann, 1987. An analysis of the revolutionary process in three political novels.

HEYWOOD, CHRISTOPHER, ed. *Perspectives on African Literature.* London: Heinemann, 1975. A discussion of the young James Ngugi and his historical roots.

JONES, ELDRED DUROSIMI, et al. *Women in African Literature Today.* Trenton, N.J.: Africa World Press, 1987. A discussion of women and resistance in *Devil on the Cross.*

KANOGO, TABITHA. *Squatters and the Roots of Mau Mau 1905–1963.* London: James Currey, 1987. A study of land alienation among the Gikuyu and the protest of the Mau Mau freedom fighters.

KENYATTA, JOMO. *Facing Mount Kenya.* New York: Vintage Books, 1965. An anthropological treatise on the Gikuyu people by Kenyatta: freedom fighter, anthropologist, and Kenya's first president.

KILLAM, G. D. *An Introduction to the Writing of Ngugi.* London: Heinemann, 1980. Criticism and analysis of Ngugi's early work.

KIRWEN, MICHAEL C. *The Missionary and the Diviner.* New York: Orbis Books, 1987. A creative dialogue comparing Christianity and traditional African religions.

LEVIN, TOBI. "Women as Scapegoats of Culture and Cult: An Activist's View of Female Circumcision in Ngugi's *The River Between*." In Carole Boyce Davies, ed., *Ngambika: Studies of Women in African Literature,* 111–148. Trenton, N.J.: Africa World Press, 1986. A discussion of Muthoni's problematic circumcision in *The River Between*.

MAINA WA KINYATTI, ed. *Kenya's Freedom Struggle: The Dedan Kimathi Papers.* London: Zed Books, 1987. Documentation of the Mau Mau movement as written by guerrilla commanders and Kimathi, including a glossary of Kikuyu words, people, and historical events; with a foreword by Ngugi wa Thiong'o.

————. *Thunder from the Mountains: Poems and Songs from the Mau Mau.* Trenton, N.J.: Africa World Press, 1990. A collection of patriotic songs and poems which were used by the freedom fighters to politicize and educate the workers and peasants of Kenya.

MBITI, JOHN. *African Religion and Philosophy.* London: Heinemann, 1969. Includes a description and analysis of the traditional cycle of life.

NAMA, CHARLES. "Daughters of Moombi: Ngugi's Heroines and Traditional Gikuyu Aesthetics." In Carole Boyce Davies, ed., *Ngambika: Studies of Women in African Literature,* 139–149. Trenton, N.J.: Africa World Press, 1986. An analysis of Ngugi's women characters.

OBIECHINA, EMMANUEL N. *Language and Theme: Essays on African Literature.* Washington, D.C.: Howard University Press, 1990. An analysis of the language issue in African literature with references to Ngugi and his work.

PALMER, EUSTACE. *An Introduction to the African Novel.* London: Heinemann, 1972. A collection of essays on Ngugi's first three novels.

PRESLEY, CORA ANN. *Kikuyu Women, the Mau Mau Rebellion, and Social Change in Kenya.* Boulder, Col.: Westview Press, 1992. A study of the Gikuyu women's contribution to social change with a focus on the Mau Mau movement and the growth of Kenyan nationalism.

RAY, BENJAMIN. "Religion and Rebellion." In *African Religions: Symbols, Ritual, and Community,* 154–173. Englewood Cliffs, N.J.: Prentice Hall, 1976. A focus on the importance of land and oath-taking rites within the Mau Mau revolution.

WILKINSON, JANE, ed. *Talking with African Writers: Interviews with African Poets, Playwrights, and Novelists.* London: Heinemann, 1992. A collection including interviews with Ngugi wa Thiong'o and Micere Githae Mugo.

A Selected Bibliography of Ngugi wa Thiongo's Work

Weep Not Child. London: Heinemann, 1964.

The River Between. London: Heinemann, 1965.

A Grain of Wheat. London: Heinemann, 1967; revised and reprinted, 1986.

The Black Hermit. London: Heinemann, 1968.

Homecoming: Essays on African and Caribbean Literature, Culture, and Politics. London: Heinemann, 1972.

Secret Lives. London: Heinemann Educational Books, 1975.

The Trial of Dedan Kimathi. Co-authored with Micere Githae Mugo. London: Heinemann African Writers Series, 1977.

Petals of Blood. London: Heinemann Educational Books, 1977; reprinted 1985.

I Will Marry When I Want. Co-authored with Ngugi wa Mirii, and translated from the Kikuyu by the authors. Nairobi: Heinemann, 1980.

Detained: A Writer's Prison Diary. London: Heinemann, 1981.

Writers in Politics. London: Heinemann, 1981.

Devil on the Cross. Translated from the Kikuyu by the author. London: Heinemann, 1982; reprinted in a new edition, 1987.

Decolonizing the Mind: The Politics of Language in African Literature. London: Heinemann, 1986.

Matigari. Translated from the Kikuyu by Wangui wa Goro. Portsmouth, N.H.: Heinemann, 1987.

Moving the Centre: The Struggle for Cultural Freedoms. Portsmouth, N.H.: Heinemann, 1993.

BOTSWANA

Kasane

Okavango River

Kalahari Desert

Francistown

Ghanzi

Motloutse River

Serowe

Lotsana River

Molopo

Tshane

Molepolole

Gaborone

0   100 kilometers

0   100 miles

Bokspits

BESSIE HEAD, A POLITICAL REFUGEE WHO MIGRATED TO BOTSWANA
FROM SOUTH AFRICA, TELLS THE STORY OF HARDWORKING PEOPLE IN
A SMALL COMMUNITY IN *WHEN RAIN CLOUDS GATHER.*

Chapter 5
▼▼▼▼▼▼▼▼▼▼▼

Bessie Head and
When Rain Clouds Gather

Bessie Head is internationally celebrated as one of southern Africa's most important writers, for her work springs from a personal and passionate understanding of the tragedy of apartheid. Published in 1968, *When Rain Clouds Gather* explores the profound patterns of evil within individuals and societies controlled by racism and prejudice. The main issues raised by the novel focus on the alienation of refugees and the transformation of life through cooperation and hard work. Makhaya Maseko, a black South African nationalist, journalist, and political exile, attempts to work with an English agriculturist in a rural haven for refugees in the heart of Botswana. He struggles with his instinctive distrust of white people, confronts oppression in the form of a local Tswana chief, and fears that freedom is merely a cruel illusion. However, through his healing relationship with the women of Golema Mmidi, Makhaya experiences the rain clouds of hope for prosperity as good people work together to build a new life. *When Rain Clouds Gather* is suitable for students on the intermediate level.

When Rain Clouds Gather and the Tswana People of Botswana
When Rain Clouds Gather, Bessie Head's first novel, celebrates the collective work of rural women as the catalyst, the driving force, and the sheer hope of future prosperity of Botswana. The author focuses on the South African refugee Makhaya Maseko and his relationships with Gilbert Balfour, Paulina Sebeso, Mma-Millipede, and the women of Golema Mmidi, as they pursue a new life through collective farming projects. As Makhaya seeks peace of mind through work, he struggles to free himself from his profound hatred of the white oppressor, and butts up against the unfamiliar force of evil in traditional Botswana leaders.

The story begins as Makhaya, a political activist, is released from a South African jail and flees across the gap of no-man's-land into the bleak and barren front-line state of Botswana. Makhaya is introduced to Golema Mmidi, a permanent settlement and safe haven for refugees. The village is primarily inhabited by women, for the men are away tending their herds at the distant cattle posts. Literally, Golema Mmidi means "to grow crops"—a difficult task for these women since Botswana has been caught in the grip of severe drought for five years, and the village's entire annual rainfall may fall in one month, one day, or even one hour.

Gilbert Balfour, an English agriculturist who is living and working with the people of Golema Mmidi, dreams of introducing new ideas and techniques that will benefit ordinary people. He envisions the cultivation, curing, and marketing of cash crops such as tobacco through cooperative farming efforts. He also hopes to introduce an extensive borehole system for irrigating the land as well as a project to improve the grade of beef by enriching the diet and restricting the grazing lands of the cattle. Gilbert knows these projects are compatible with traditional communal ownership of the land and are necessary for survival. However, he is opposed by the local Tswana chief, Matenge, who maintains that he alone has the right to regulate economic development. Gilbert also perceives the Tswana women as the foundation of the agricultural base and the hope of the future. Therefore, he offers Makhaya a position teaching the village women the fundamentals of sound agricultural techniques and asks him to introduce the concept of cultivating and curing tobacco.

Gilbert and Makhaya are opposed by Chief Matenge and his servant, Joas Tsepe, the undersecretary general of the Botswana National Liberation Party. Gilbert's cooperative ventures have broken Matenge's monopoly on the cattle business and allowed ordinary co-op members to receive fair prices for their cattle. Furthermore, other African leaders, such as Matenge's brother, the paramount chief Sekoto, tolerate but do not understand Gilbert's concern for the poor. As royalty, Matenge and his kinsmen believe that ordinary people deserve to be poor.

As Makhaya struggles with life in an unfamiliar country, he grapples with the concepts of good and evil and attempts to overcome his hatred of the white man by developing a relationship with Gilbert. Mma-Millipede, an elderly village woman, extends her hand in friendship and confirms Makhaya's belief that life's most crucial component is generosity to others. Because Makhaya considers himself the "Black Dog" of apartheid, he rejects the oppressive white civilization ushered in by double-talking Christian ministers. Nevertheless, he discovers human compassion through his relationship with Gilbert and attempts to combine the fine qualities he finds in his friend with the good elements of African society.

The initial setting and conflict in the novel reflect the history of several ethnic groups in southern Africa. Botswana is the home of the San and the Khoi, ancient indigenous peoples who lived on the fringe of the Kalahari desert. The San were peaceful hunters and gatherers who valued poets and singers and developed a remarkable form of rock art by recording scenes of daily life in vivid colors on cave walls. The Khoi were cattle herders who grad-ually absorbed the San, and the amalgamated group became known as the Khoisan.

The Tswana are a Sotho group of Bantu speakers who migrated from East Africa and gradually displaced or absorbed the Khoisan. Originally united, the Tswana soon divided into independent chiefdoms which varied in size and composition. The chief was the dominant political figure in Tswana society and controlled internal economic activity by supervising the allocation of land during the annual agricultural cycle, regulating trade, and presiding over religious rites such as rainmaking.

The Tswana chiefdoms grew as nearby ethnic groups were conquered; the Tswana also granted refugees asylum and admitted other people as im-migrants. As a result, Tswana society basically consisted of four social classes. The royal class included the kinsmen of the chief, and the commoner class included groups of people who had been incorporated into the community long ago. The lower class consisted of refugees and recent immigrant groups, and the lowest class was the serfs, or the Masarwa. These descendants of the Khoisan were treated as slaves, enjoyed few privileges, and were de-pendent upon a ruling family.

The core of Tswana society was the town. The principal town in an area was inhabited by the chief and his ruling community; other towns were actually clusters of villages inhabited by the royal class and commoners. Al-though the town was a hub of activity, it was abandoned from October to May each year as Tswana families relocated to nearby agricultural lands in order to cultivate and harvest the year's crop. During this time, the head of the family and his adult sons also spent several weeks working at the cattle posts, which were scattered around the countryside.

In *When Rain Clouds Gather*, Gilbert Balfour and Makhaya Maseko at-tempt to revolutionize traditional Tswana subsistence farming techniques in Golema Mmidi by introducing Turkish tobacco as a cash crop. However, the only one in the village capable of persuading the other women to learn new agricultural techniques is the strong-willed Paulina Sebeso. Although Makhaya initially spurns Paulina's gesture of friendship, he soon recognizes that her unique and daring brand of leadership is crucial to his project.

Through Paulina's organization and supervision, all one hundred and fifty women in the village commit themselves to building tobacco sheds and cultivating the new crop. The project should produce the capital needed to set up networks of underground water boreholes resulting in reservoirs in Golema Mmidi. Every household would have water, vegetable gardens would flourish, and irrigation schemes allowing cattle to graze near the vil-lage could be implemented. Under Paulina's leadership, Golema Mmidi holds the promise of becoming the greatest tobacco-producing area in the country and a model for other villages.

However, in spite of the villagers' hard work and achievements, Golema Mmidi is soon overcome by severe drought. Scorching winds, huge swirling pillars of red desert dust, and intense stifling heat engulf the country in August. September is the month when rain clouds always gather in the sky, but this year it brings no clouds at all and no hope of rain. Gradually the cattle in the isolated posts begin dropping dead one by one. For the first time in living memory, the cattle are simply overcome by thirst and perish, emaciated after eating nothing but dry, brittle grass for ten months.

Paulina had entrusted her herd to the care of her ten-year-old son, Isaac, who was slowly dying of tuberculosis at his cold, isolated post. When Gilbert, Makhaya, and Paulina finally arrive at the cattle post, the small boy is dead—his flesh destroyed by white ants and maggots. As Paulina grieves and desperately blames herself for her son's tragic death, she is called to court by Chief Matenge. Knowing that he intends to prosecute Paulina for Isaac's death—a death caused by the drought and famine that is plaguing the country—the entire village rises in support and accompanies Paulina to Matenge's mansion. As the ordinary people of the village surround his citadel, Matenge panics. It seems as if the collective will of the people somehow extinguishes the evil of Matenge, the corrupt leader who is obstructing progress for the poor.

The people of Botswana demonstrate the spirit of hope in the face of drought, famine, persecution, and death. The rain clouds that gather in their hearts symbolize hope for new life. It is in this spirit that Makhaya and Paulina join hands. Their union indicates that rain clouds of hope have indeed gathered, for these refugees stand as a promise of new life and prosperity through hard work and cooperation in Botswana.

Literary Techniques in When Rain Clouds Gather
The novel is set in the refugee village of Golema Mmidi in Botswana near the northern border of South Africa. Golema Mmidi is a relatively new settlement made up of outcasts who have nowhere to go—outcasts who are willing to work hard to create a new life out of nothing. The events in the novel take place just before the Bechuanaland Protectorate achieved independence from Britain in 1966 and became known as Botswana.

As a person of mixed ancestry, Bessie Head herself is a refugee and an outcast of South African society. She addresses her own experience of a refugee's alienation and hope for a new life in *When Rain Clouds Gather.* The author's interest in the relationships among people are illustrated through the friendships of Dinorego, Mma-Millipede, Gilbert, Paulina, and Makhaya. The women of the community are also presented as workers capable of pitching themselves into difficult, labor-intensive work with joy and the spirit of camaraderie.

Vivid imagery is a technique that illustrates the relationship between people and the environment. For example, the author shows how the hearts of the men of Botswana are heavy as she vividly describes their terrible view of the cattle posts strewn with the carcasses of emaciated cattle overcome by thirst. The author graphically describes the result of too many bitterly cold nights in the bush on Isaac, the ten-year-old boy who has become nothing but a heap of small white bones on the floor of his camp—his flesh destroyed by the white ants and maggots who had feasted on his tiny body.

Furthermore, the author skillfully connects the crops planted, the drought, and new methods of agriculture with the attitudes of society. She explains how the drought-resistant millet, which is the traditional food of the Kalahari Khoisan people, is not accepted by the ruling Tswana community, for the leaders are blinded by prejudice. Various aspects of authority such as the power of traditional chiefs, the attitudes of the new politicians, and the authority of the working people of Botswana themselves are also explored in relationship to agriculture and the cattle industry. Like her heroine Paulina, the author holds up the symbol of rain clouds of hope as she retells the story of cooperation, generosity, and hard work in the new Botswana.

Finally, throughout the novel, images of horror become images of new life as the spirit of alienation gives way to peace and prosperity. For example, the police sirens that pierce the night in pursuit of Makhaya are juxtaposed with the tinkling of the cattle's bells as the fugitive initially enters the safe zone of Botswana. Similarly, toward the end of the novel, the dynamite that Makhaya uses to blast boreholes and create an irrigation system for the community takes the place of the explosives he intended to detonate in the faces of his white oppressors in South Africa.

Points to Ponder

The question of character may focus on Makhaya. He is a South African fugitive who is an instrument of new life. Initially in his despair and loneliness, Makhaya is faced with the challenge of the British agriculturist Gilbert Balfour who hires him to mobilize refugee women to grow Turkish tobacco—one of the easiest and most profitable cash crops for the people of Golema Mmidi. Although Makhaya accepts the position, he perceives himself as the "Black Dog" of apartheid and does not trust Gilbert. How does Makhaya's relationship with Mma-Millipede change his attitude? What qualities does Makhaya see in Paulina that confirm his instincts about generosity and hard work? How does the healing touch of these women help him rediscover human compassion and the will to live? How is the entire novel a metaphor of optimism and hope?

Other issues concern the profound patterns of good and evil within individuals and societies controlled by racism and prejudice. How is the corruption and greed of Chief Matenge, Joas Tsepe, and the paramount chief Sekoto in contrast with the hard work and generosity of the refugees of

Golema Mmidi? Why does Chief Matenge attempt to hold Paulina responsible for the death of Isaac? In what way is the chief himself responsible for
the innocent boy's demise?

The portrayal of women as individuals and as a collective work force is
another important point to ponder. Is the character of Paulina realistic in her
strength and ability to introduce new ideas? How do the women of the community organize themselves and set the pulse of life in the village through
their solidarity and labor? What are the attitudes of the women to love, marriage, work, and death? How do Paulina, Maria, and Mma-Millipede comple-
ment one another, and how are these characters different?

Finally, what is the significance of the title of the novel? What happens
in Botswana when rain clouds gather? For example, how would you finish
this sentence: "When rain clouds gather, . . . "? Maria, Gilbert Balfour's stoic
bride, explains that although the people of Botswana may not see rivers of
water coursing through the land, rivers flow within the hearts of the hope-
ful. As all good people and all good things are called *pula* or rain, the Tswana
often see rain clouds gathering even though nothing at all appears in the
sky. What is the nature of hope for the people of Botswana? Are the rain
clouds of the novel realistic, or are these clouds simply empty dreams of displaced outcasts in a barren land?

Another discussion may focus on the concept of rain. What is the significance and power of rain for the Tswana people, and why do the Tswana
have such a great respect for rain clouds? As historically agricultural people
who also managed large herds of cattle in a bleak environment, was the survival of the Tswana tied to the rain? How is the concept of rain manifest in
the language and everyday greetings of the people? What kinds of rain do
the people pray for, and historically, what was the relationship of rainmaking
to traditional political authority? Finally, how has the history of rainmaking
changed with the introduction of new agricultural methods, irrigation, and
Christianity? A more in-depth understanding of the concept of rain within
the Tswana world view may be helpful in addressing these issues.

Rain and Rain Clouds in the Traditional Tswana World View

Botswana borders the Kalahari desert; as a result, annual rainfall is scant, unre-
liable, and subject to high rates of evaporation and drainage. Because the land
is often plagued by drought, the Tswana people have always been intensely
interested in the subject of rain. Many believe water is the rarest and most
precious substance on earth and consider rain crucial for agricultural production and the care of cattle. The concepts of rain and well-being are synony-
mous in the Tswana world view, and the term *pula* describes both. *Pula* is also
the basic Tswana greeting. Derivations of *pula* are used as names for children
born during the rains, and the Tswana thank one another by saying,
Kkegonesa pula, "May it rain for you." One wishes a companion a good jour-

ney by saying, *Tsamaya kapula,* "Go with rain," and *Goroga kapula,* "Return with rain."

Traditional Tswana cosmology describes two basic types of rain. *Pula ya medupe* is white rain; this is the gentle, benevolent, soaking rain that nurtures the agricultural and pastoral lands. *Pula ya dikadima* is violent bursts of rain accompanied by thunder and lightning; this fierce rain frightens animals and people, damages crops, erodes the soil, and evaporates without nurturing the land.

The Tswana people respect and understand rain as a sacred element of fertility and prosperity, and they believe that only the supreme god Modimo can actually make rain. However, the Tswana believe that traditional medicine produced with careful knowledge of certain plants and trees allowed rainmakers to charm the clouds and beg the ancestral spirits of deceased chiefs to intercede for rain. Rainmaking was essentially a religious rite, and smoke from the rain pots acted like incense, giving efficacy to the power of the people's prayers.

Historically, rainmaking also played an important role in Tswana politics, for the subjects of the various chiefdoms perceived the chief as the principal rainmaker ritually responsible for forming rain clouds in the sky. Many of the ceremonies were performed in the rain kraal and involved burning and stirring medicines in rain pots in order to summon rain clouds. Other rites were precautionary and aimed as preventing the occurrence of drought or the transformation of rain into hail. Various rain ceremonies and rites were generally performed at the beginning of the rainy season and again later in the year if necessary. Rain was a constant preoccupation in Tswana society. Rain was so important that it was customary for the chief to begin and end his political addresses to the people throughout the year by saying, "Let it rain!" The people would response in a cheering chorus, "*Pula! Pula!*" ("Rain! Rain!")

As the Tswana became Christianized, the traditional rainmaking rites gradually became consolidated in Christian days of prayer for rain organized by the chief and the church at the beginning of the cultivating season. To this day, the Tswana people maintain a profound understanding and respect for the great mystery of rain. Their insight is revealed in many proverbs and constant references to rain. For example, the Tswana will tell you, "Although smoke is a sign of fire, clouds are not always a sign of rain."

The Author and Her Work

Bessie Head

Throughout her life, Bessie Head experienced the racism and prejudice of the apartheid system in South Africa and the joys and sorrows of life as a refugee in Botswana. Bessie Head's maternal grandparents, Thomas and Alice Birch, emigrated to South Africa from England in 1892 and settled in the Orange Free State. Their daughter, Bessie Birch, who was nicknamed Toby, married an Australian immigrant named Ira Emery and gave birth to

PAULINA STANDS FOR THE RAIN CLOUDS OF HOPE IN GOLEMA MMIDI.

two sons, Stanley and Ronald. Tragedy struck however, as four-year-old Stanley was killed by a car in front of his mother's very eyes. Toby Emery never recovered from the shock, and her marriage soon resulted in divorce. Eight years later, Toby was admitted to Fort Napier Institution for the mentally ill in Pietermaritzburg; she was seven months pregnant, and the father of her child was unknown. Two months later on July 6, 1937, Toby Emery gave birth to a daughter whom she named Bessie Amelia Emery. Little Bessie was adopted by a white South African family but soon returned, for the child was perceived to be "Colored," appearing to be somewhat African in appearance. Bessie was then placed with Nellie and George Heathcote, who received a monthly payment for raising Bessie. When little Bessie was six years old, her mother, Toby Emery, who was suffering from severe schizophrenia, died at the age of forty-seven due to an abscess in her lungs.

Young Bessie Emery grew up believing herself to be the daughter of Nellie Heathcote and was distraught when, at the age of thirteen, she was placed in St. Monica's Home, an Anglican Mission school for "Colored" girls. Here the headmistress cruelly explained that Bessie's real mother was white and insane; her father was African. Bessie then believed that her mother was from the wealthy Birch family well known for its racehorses; she believed her father was the family's stablehand. This in fact was not true, for Bessie Emery's ancestors were not the wealthy Birches but another Birch family of much more modest means who did not own racehorses or maintain a stable.

In 1954 a compassionate woman named Margaret Cadmore became the headmistress of St. Monica's School, and she assisted Bessie with her studies and encouraged her to teach. Two years later, Bessie took a position at the Clairwood Colored School. She soon moved into journalism, however, and worked with the *Golden City Post* in Cape Town and Johannesburg. In 1961, after a brief courtship, Bessie married the journalist Harold Head. A year later their son, Howard Head, was born, and the family moved to Port Elizabeth. However, Bessie grew increasingly unhappy in her marriage and found life in the racist South Africa intolerable. In 1964, she accepted a teaching position in the village of Serowe in Bechuanaland and left South Africa with her two-year-old son on a one-way exit permit. Six months later, Harold Head fled from South Africa and followed Bessie to Bechuanaland; he finally emigrated to Canada.

Although Bessie Head was a naturally talented journalist, she was not a successful teacher. She soon left her position and moved on to the Bamangwato Development Farm which was dedicated to improving agricultural methods. After leaving the farm, she landed in a refugee settlement in Francistown. Finally, in 1969, Bessie returned to Serowe. However, she was not granted Botswana citizenship and was held in refugee status for the next ten years.

Bessie Head lived in simple, abject poverty, struggling to make ends meet in a variety of ways. She carried on a voluminous correspondence and often wrote for long hours by candlelight. Bessie was emotionally volatile, experienced several nervous breakdowns, and according to some sources, slipped in and out of madness. Nevertheless, her creative energy was channeled into her work. She wrote short stories and articles which were published in a variety of magazines and journals, and in 1968 she published her first novel, *When Rain Clouds Gather*, which was drawn from her experiences on the Bamangwato Development Farm. Two years later she published *Maru*, which reflected her difficult teaching career at the Tshekedi Memorial School in Serowe. Later, she suffered a severe nervous breakdown, which was recorded in her autobiographical masterpiece titled *A Question of Power*, published in 1974. A collection of stories titled *The Collector of Treasures and Other Botswana Village Tales* followed in 1977 and focused on the courage of women.

Over the course of the next five years, Bessie participated in a variety of projects including the international writing program held at the University of Iowa in 1977. In 1979, after finally receiving Botswana citizenship, she attended the Berlin Festival of World Cultures, and in 1980 she traveled to Denmark to celebrate the seventy-fifth anniversary of the Danish Library Association. She participated in television programs sponsored by development organizations in the Netherlands, and in 1982 she traveled to Nigeria where she gave a keynote address with Ngugi wa Thiong'o at the University of Calabar's International Conference on African Literature. In 1981 Bessie Head published *Serowe: Village of the Rain Wind*, a collection of interviews focusing on nearly a century of educational activities in Botswana including the Swaneng Project in which she participated. And, in 1984, after almost ten years of historical research, she finally published her historical novel titled *A Bewitched Crossroad: An African Saga*, which retells the history of southern Africa as it focuses on the people of Botswana and their great leader Khama III.

Suddenly, in March of 1986 Bessie fell ill and was diagnosed with hepatitis. Her liver malfunctioned, and she slipped into unconsciousness. Tragically, Bessie Head passed away a month later on April 17, 1986, at the age of forty-nine. The literary world was shocked by this great and unexpected loss. Nevertheless, the creative work of Bessie Head continued to be published posthumously. In 1989 over twenty stories were collected in *Tales of Tenderness and Power*; in 1990 *A Woman Alone: Autobiographical Writings* was edited by Craig MacKenzie. In 1991 Randolph Vigne also edited a volume entitled *A Gesture of Belonging: Letters from Bessie Head, 1965–1979*. Finally, in 1993, a novella recording Bessie Head's experiences in Cape Town and written in the early 1960s was published posthumously as *The Cardinals*.

Bessie Head's Work

Bessie Head's first novel, *When Rain Clouds Gather*, was published in 1968; this was followed by *Maru* in 1971. *Maru* focuses on the deep-rooted prejudice and discrimination experienced by the descendants of the ancient Khoisan, who are pejoratively known as Bushmen by white colonists or Masarwa by the people of Botswana. The Masarwa were attached to the Tswana groups as bonded slaves and, although they were granted human rights by Khama III, they remained a subjugated minority. The protagonist of the novel, Margaret Cadmore, is a well-educated teacher who appears to be "Colored" but who wrecks havoc in the remote village of Dilepe when she declares herself to be a Masarwa. Two prominent Tswana leaders fall in love with Margaret: Maru, the young paramount chief elect, and his close companion, Moleka. Margaret struggles to understand the unjust society she faces and, befriended by Maru's capable sister, Dikeledi, retreats into her own world of art and creative expression. Her insightful, sensitive drawings open her world up to Maru. The young Tswana leader becomes god-like as he renounces his position in order to marry Margaret and identify himself, his power, and his prestige with the slaves of humankind. The name "Maru" literally translates as the black, brooding storm clouds that remain trapped like prisoners along the horizon. Just as these dark clouds do not hold the promise of life-giving rain and prosperity, nor does the novel offer resolution to the bitterness of racism and prejudice. However, *Maru* explores the deep roots of racism and focuses on the dialogue between the oppressor and the oppressed.

Bessie Head records other aspects of her life and claims to tell an impossible story about the sources and patterns of evil in *A Question of Power*, her autobiographical masterpiece which was published in 1974. The novel is an allegory about Bessie Head's nervous breakdown and is framed by the journey of three companions into the depths of hell. Elizabeth represents Bessie herself, for as an orphan and racial outcast born of a white South African mother and a black South African father, she carries the stigma of madness inherited from her mother, who committed suicide in an insane asylum. Her story is framed by her experience as a refugee struggling to adapt to rural African society and participate in a development scheme. Sello and Dan accompany Elizabeth on her journey into hell. Sello, who is at one time wise, human, and loving, fragments into characters such as Medusa and Father. Medusa is an evil figure that may represent dimensions of Elizabeth herself; Father may represent the traditional image of God. Sello attains positions of power from which he has perpetrated many evil actions in the name of God. Dan also uses power in a dangerous and destructive way. He may in fact represent Lucifer, who matches his supernatural power with the power of God. Contending that Elizabeth is not truly an African and therefore cannot respond sexually, Dan torments her with sexual hype and hysteria. Overall, Elizabeth learns that love is not the cannibalistic feeding of one upon another but rather a mutual and compassionate act of nurturing. As Elizabeth gradually recovers from her nervous breakdown and nightmarish descent into hell, she chooses to serve others and forces herself to overcome her feelings of isolation and alienation in society. She has walked the thin line between good and evil and concludes that if these forces are truly "a question of power," then power causes evil, and love and goodness are devoid of the power to control and coerce. Elizabeth seems to have achieved some measure of peace, for as the novel ends, her ability to nurture her son is re-established. In the final lines, she falls asleep and extends her hand over her new land in a quiet gesture of acceptance and belonging.

In 1977, Bessie Head published a collection of short stories entitled *The Collector of Treasures and Other Botswana Village Tales*. This work captures many dimensions of Botswana history and village life and focuses on courage, compassion, and the relationships between men and women. The stories are arranged to illustrate various and increasingly complex relationships between husbands and wives. "The Deep River: A Story of Ancient Tribal Migration" reveals a chief who chooses the woman he loves rather than traditional power. In other stories, a faith-healing priest is supported by his devoted wife, and heaven is held open for a woman who attempts to compromise Christianity and traditional beliefs. In "Looking for a Rain God," a drought-ridden community remains compassionate and empathizes with a family who desperately searches for rain and practices forbidden rites in order to survive. In "Witchcraft," the moral fiber of courageous women is celebrated as Mma-Mabele dispels the darkness of superstition and fear, and in "The Collector of Treasures," Dikeledi Mokopi, a prisoner who is supported by a strong African sisterhood, takes justice into her own hands and summons the will to live amid oppression.

Serowe: Village of the Rain Wind was published in 1981 and is a remarkable collection of nearly one hundred interviews with the people of Serowe. Through the words of these villagers, the truths and complexities of reforming the traditional order in Botswana emerge. The interviews focus on social reform and educational progress during three distinct time periods: the long reign of Khama the Great, which spanned 1875–1923; the era of Tshekedi Khama and Seretse Khama, which spanned 1926–1959; and the Swaneng educational project, which was instituted in 1963 by Patrick van Rensburg. The villagers explain that the old traditional order was systematically reconstructed under the personal supervision of Khama III. During Tshekedi's and Seretse's time, the powerful Bamangwato chieftaincy itself was replaced by emerging political parties, and educational and social reform continued through the Swaneng project, organized by Patrick van Rensburg.

In 1984, after ten years of research, Bessie Head published a novel entitled *A Bewitched Crossroad: An African Saga*, which depicts the history of the southern African region during the nineteenth century. The story is told through a fictional Tswana chief named Sebina and focuses on the great struggle of divergent peoples to control the land. The African migrations are depicted as the Zulu warrior king Shaka and the Matabele king Mzilikazi reconfigure the face of Africa, while the Moshoeshoe offers a haven for refugees in Lesotho. The migrations of the Boers result in the establishment of the Orange Free State and the Transvaal, two republics that defy British authority and declare a fundamental right to own African slaves. British missionaries like John MacKenzie become diplomatic emissaries for the Tswana people, and gold and diamonds are discovered in the region. The diamond magnate Cecil Rhodes establishes the South African Company, tricks Mzilikazi's successor, Lobengula, into signing away his lands through the Rudd concession, and attempts to take over Bechuanaland (Botswana). Throughout this historical African saga of political instability, a monumental figure emerges in Khama the Great of the Bamangwato people. This austere, Christianized Tswana leader reforms traditional practices, and works with Sebele and Bathoen of neighboring chiefdoms to secure continued British protection for Bechuanaland. The great Khama III, who is portrayed as the austere "Mother Winter" of the Bamangwato praise poems, maintains the land of his people, giving up only a narrow strip on the eastern border for a railway line linking the interior with the Cape. As African peoples are stripped of their lands and human rights, the Tswana stand on a "bewitched crossroad," and Bechuanaland remains a black man's country where the rhythm of life pulses on.

Bessie Head published numerous short stories in various magazines and journals throughout her lifetime; over twenty of these stories were published posthumously in 1989 in a collection entitled *Tales of Tenderness and Power*. The stories include "The Woman from America," which had been published in *The New Statesman* in 1966, and "Chibuku Beer and Independence," which celebrates the calm questioning peace surrounding an independence ceremony in Botswana. A series of historical tales, including "A Period of Darkness" and the traditional story of "The Lovers," reflect Bessie's historical research on the Tswana people. Finally, "The Prisoner Who Wore Glasses," one of her best known and most often anthologized stories, is included along with "The Coming of the Christ Child," a tribute to the integrity of an ideal political leader.

A Woman Alone: Autobiographical Writings was edited by Craig MacKenzie and published in 1990. This collection of journalism, autobiographical sketches, letters, essays, stories, and explanatory notes begins to tell the story of Bessie Head's life. The work is divided into three sections. The first spans 1937 to 1964 and includes writings about her family background, difficult childhood, failed marriage, and experience in the ghettos of South Africa. The second section focuses on her exile in Botswana from 1964 to 1979. During her severe nervous breakdown, she publicly accused President Seretse Khama of incest and ritual cannibalism. She was taken into psychiatric custody and later recorded her descent into hell in *A Question of Power*. The third section of these autobiographical writings reflects Bessie Head's life as a Botswana citizen from 1979 to 1984, a happier time during which she enjoyed international success as a writer and was invited to the official exhibition of "Writers of Botswana" in Gaborone.

Throughout her lifetime, Bessie Head carried on a voluminous and lively correspondence with her publishers, agents, literary contacts, and friends all over the world. Trained as a journalist, she kept carbon copies of her correspondence and classified the letters she received. In 1991, Randolph Vigne, a journalist and activist who had worked with Bessie and Harold Head in South Africa, published approximately one hundred letters he received from Bessie in a volume entitled *A Gesture of Belonging: Letters from Bessie Head, 1965–1979*. These letters are a fraction of the several thousand letters which were written and received by Bessie Head and which are stored in the Bessie Head archive in Serowe.

Finally, *The Cardinals, with Meditations and Short Stories* was published posthumously in 1993. *The Cardinals* was actually Bessie Head's first lengthy fictional piece and was written in South Africa during the early 1960s. The story focuses on the Immorality Act of the 1950s, which condemned sexual unions between people of different races. The protagonist, a beautiful young woman named Mouse, is an illegitimate half-caste who lives in District Six, a "Colored" slum in Cape Town. As Mouse explores forbidden love, the relationship between sex and death, and the injustices of life in South Africa, she defines herself through the act of creative writing.

Resources

CAMERON, TREWHELLA, ed. *A New Illustrated History of South Africa.* Johannesburg: Southern Book Publishers, 1986. A detailed illustrated history including the story of the first peoples of southern Africa.

COUNDOURIOTIS, ELENI. "Authority and Invention in the Fiction of Bessie Head." *Research in African Literatures* 27, 2 (Summer 1996): 17–32. An analysis of Bessie Head's explicit portrayal of the relationship between authority and authorship in *Maru* and *A Question of Power.*

EILERSEN, GILLIAN STEAD. *Bessie Head—Thunder Behind Her Ears.* Portsmouth, N.H.: Heinemann, 1995. An extensive study of Head's life and works.

GARDNER, SUSAN, and PATRICIA E. SCOTT. *Bessie Head: A Bibliography.* Grahamstown, South Africa. National Literary Museum, 1986. A bibliography of Head's writing and criticism of her work including an excellent introduction.

GRAY, STEPHEN, ed. *Modern South African Stories.* Johannesburg: A.D. Donker, 1980. A collection of twenty-eight stories by writers intimately concerned with modern South Africa, including "The Prisoner who Wore Glasses."

————. *The Penguin Book of Southern African Stories.* New York: Viking Penguin, 1986. A collection of stories, including "The Lovers."

HARROW, KENNETH. "Change on the Margins." In *Thresholds of Change in African Literature: The Emergence of a Tradition,* 195–208. Portsmouth, N.H.: Heinemann, 1994. An insightful discussion of Head's short stories in *A Collector of Treasures.*

HIRSON, DENIS, and MARTIN TRUMP, eds. *The Heinemann Book of South African Short Stories from 1945 to the Present.* Portsmouth, N.H.: Heinemann, 1994. A collection of South African stories, including "The Prisoner Who Wore Glasses."

MACKENZIE, CRAIG. *Bessie Head: An Introduction.* Grahamstown, South Africa: National Literary Museum, 1989. A basic overview of Head's life and work.

MACKENZIE, CRAIG, and CHERRY CLAYTON, eds. *Between the Lines: Interviews with Bessie Head.* Grahamstown, South Africa: National Literary Museum, 1989. Interviews collected by Sheila Roberts, Ellen Kuzwayo, and Miriam Tlali.

OLAOGUN, MODUPE O. "Irony and Schizophrenia in Bessie Head's *Maru.*" *Research in African Literatures* 25, 4 (Winter 1994): 69–87. An exploration of Maru and Moleka and how these two male characters relate as one to Margaret Cadmore in *Maru.*

OMER-COOPER, J. D. *History of Southern Africa.* Portsmouth, N.H.: Heinemann, 1994. A detailed history of the region.

PHILLIPS, MAGGI. "Engaging Dreams: Alternative Perspectives on Flora Nwapa, Buchi Emecheta, Ama Ata Aidoo, Bessie Head, and Tsitsi Dangarembga's Writing." *Research in African Literatures* 25, 4 (Winter 1994): 89–103. A comparative analysis of dreams in African women's writing.

SARVAN, CHARLES PONNUTHURAI. "Bessie Head: *A Question of Power* and Identity."

In E. D. Jones, ed., *Women in African Literature Today*, 82–88. Trenton, N.J.: Africa World Press, 1987. An analysis of the writer and her identification within the novel.

SCANLON, PAUL, ed. *Stories from Central and Southern Africa*. Portsmouth, N.H.: Heinemann, 1989. A collection of short stories from Mozambique, Zimbabwe, Botswana, Lesotho, Swaziland, Malawi, Namibia, and South Africa, including "Witchcraft" by Bessie Head.

SCHAPERA, ISAAC. *Rainmaking Rites of Tswana Tribes*. Leiden: Afrika-Studiecentrum, 1971. A study of the beliefs and practices associated with rainmaking among the Tswana people of southeastern Botswana, including an analysis of rainfall and the economy, the politics and art of rainmaking, and rituals.

———. *Tribal Innovators: Tswana Chiefs and Social Change, 1795–1940*. New York: Humanities Press, 1970. Analysis of the changes instituted by Tswana chiefs through 1940.

SCHAPERA, ISAAC, and JOHN COMAROFF. *The Tswana*. London and New York: Paul Kegan International in Association with International African Institute, 1991. An overview of the Tswana people from 1900 through 1985 with chapters on history, language, literature, economy, society, religion, and political organization.

SHILLINGTON, KEVIN. *A History of Southern Africa*. London: Longman Press, 1993. A comprehensive history beginning with the peopling of southern Africa and extending to the twentieth-century challenge to colonialism.

THOMPSON, LEONARD. *A History of South Africa*. New Haven: Yale University Press, 1995. A comprehensive history of South Africa including excellent illustrations and an important chapter on the transition period from 1989–1995.

A Selected Bibliography of Bessie Head's Work

When Rain Clouds Gather. New York: Simon and Schuster, 1968; Portsmouth, N.H.: Heinemann, 1987.

Maru. London: Gollancz, 1971; New York: McCall, 1971; Portsmouth, N.H.: Heinemann, 1987.

A Question of Power. London: Davis Poynter, 1974; London and Portsmouth, N.H.: Heinemann, 1974.

The Collector of Treasures and Other Botswana Village Tales. London: Heinemann, 1977; Portsmouth, N.H.: Heinemann, 1992.

Serowe: Village of the Rain Wind. London and Portsmouth, N.H.: Heinemann, 1981.

A Bewitched Crossroad: An African Saga. Craighall, South Africa: A. D. Donker, 1984.

Tales of Tenderness and Power. Craighall, South Africa: A. D. Donker, 1989; Portsmouth, N.H.: Heinemann, 1989.

A Woman Alone: Autobiographical Writings. Edited by Craig MacKenzie. London and Portsmouth, N.H.: Heinemann, 1990.

A Gesture of Belonging: Letters from Bessie Head, 1965–1979. Edited by Randolph Vigne. London: SA Writers, 1991; London and Portsmouth, N.H.: Heinemann, 1991.

The Cardinals, with Meditations and Short Stories. Edited by M. J. Daymond. Southern Africa: David Philip Publishers, 1993; London and Portsmouth, N.H.: Heinemann, 1995.

SOUTH AFRICA

ALEX LA GUMA'S WORK REVEALS VARIOUS DIMENSIONS OF THE
FREEDOM STRUGGLE IN SOUTH AFRICA. THE CHARACTERS IN *TIME OF
THE BUTCHERBIRD* INHABIT THE GREAT KAROO.

Chapter 6
▼▼▼▼▼▼▼▼▼▼▼

Alex La Guma and
Time of the Butcherbird

As a member of the South African Colored Peoples' Congress, undersecretary of the African National Congress, political prisoner, and exile, Alex La Guma's creative writing reflects his commitment to justice. *Time of the Butcherbird*, published in 1979, provides a social history of South Africa. The issues raised by the novel are rooted in centuries of injustice as the Afrikaner government enforces the Group Areas Act and attempts to move black South Africans into impoverished Bantustans. The conflict centers on the relationship between the African worker Shilling Murile and the Afrikaner farmer Hannes Meulen. As Shilling Murile avenges himself through violence, he acts like the butcherbird who cleanses the cattle of bloodsucking ticks. Like Shilling, the South African majority is called to organized armed resistance in order to purge the land of injustice. *Time of the Butcherbird* is appropriate for students on the intermediate or advanced levels in English and social studies classes. The novel can be used effectively in a unit on the history and literature of South Africa, or in a unit on apartheid and the freedom struggle of the African National Congress.

Time of the Butcherbird and the Peoples of South Africa
Three major segments of South African society are represented in *Time of the Butcherbird*: the powerful Afrikaner population, the disenfranchised poor consisting of black and mixed-race ethnic groups, and the English community. The Afrikaners are represented by Hannes Meulen; his grandfather, Oupa Meulen; his fiancée, Rina Steen; and his assistant, Jaap Opperman. The non-white population of South Africa is represented by the people of the Karoo. They include Shilling Murile; his brother, Timi Murile; the shepherd Madonele; the headman Hlangeni; and Hlangeni's militant sister, Mma-Tau. The English population is represented by the traveling salesman Edgar Stopes; his wife, Maisie; and her parents, the Barends. Three plots emerge and are woven together throughout the book. The first is the personal conflict between Hannes Meulen and Shilling Murile; the second is

99
▼

the mass removal of Hlangeni's people from their ancestral lands to a deserted Bantustan; and the third is the failed marriage of Edgar Stopes.

Hannes Meulen and his family represent three generations of Afrikaner history in South Africa. The elder Oupa Meulen settled in the Karoo area in the 1800s and represents the Dutch settlers who trekked inland from the Cape, annihilating the Khoisan people, seizing the land of other indigenous peoples, and imposing the belief that the Afrikaners were God's chosen race in Africa. The generation of Oupa's son, Christofel Meulen, further develops the Afrikaner culture and carves the land into large sheep farms. Oupa's grandson, Hannes, carries on the family tradition, for he is an elected official who represents the capitalist interests of the Afrikaners in the Karoo and works with authorities to ensure the mass removal of the black population. Hannes' betrothed, the beautiful Rina, represents the ideal Afrikaner woman—one who will preserve the culture by rearing children who believe in their God-given superiority over other ethnic groups.

Shilling Murile is employed on Hannes Meulen's farm. Shilling's people have inhabited the Karoo for centuries—since the early 1600s, before the Dutch first arrived at the Cape of Good Hope. Shilling and his brother, Timi, are asked to serve at the wedding celebration of Hannes' sister Berti. They become intoxicated and invite the sheep to dance. The sheep escape, and the brothers are accused of theft. They are lashed to a fence by Hannes Meulen and Jaap Opperman, and Timi dies of exposure in the long winter night. As Shilling is released in the morning, he slashes Jaap's arm with a broken bottle. A judge sentences him to ten years of hard labor in prison for attempted murder, and simply fines Hannes Meulen for causing Timi's death. As the novel opens, Shilling has served eight years in prison and is returning to the Meulen farm to avenge his brother's death.

The first section of the novel recalls the histories of various indigenous peoples of South Africa and those peoples who migrated to South Africa, including the Khoisan, Ndebele, Sotho, Xhosa, and Zulu, as well as the Afrikaners, Indonesians, and British. The earliest identified people groups of the region were the San and the Khoi, who inhabited the southernmost areas of Africa during the Late Stone Age. Other African peoples including the Swazi, Ndebele, Xhosa, and Zulu settled in the northern and eastern areas of South Africa about the fourth century A.D.

The Afrikaner and Indonesian populations arrived in South Africa during the seventeenth century through the Europeans' quest for sea routes to the East. In 1652, the Dutch East India Company built a small fort at the Cape of Good Hope in order to maintain water supplies, cultivate gardens of fresh vegetables, and serve as a refreshment station for the trading company's crews. In time, many employees detached themselves from the company and became independent farmers. These people, who were later known as the Boers or Afrikaners, waged war with the Khoisan. In 1658 the Afrikaners began to import slaves from the Dutch East Indies, and through the intermarriage of slaves and Afrikaners, the so-called "Cape Colored" population was produced. The Boers also assimilated the French and Belgian Huguenots who introduced the doctrine of the elect, which identified the Afrikaners as the chosen people of God. As the seventeenth century drew to an end, the histories of the Afrikaner and African peoples were inextricably and tragically bound in South Africa.

During the eighteenth century the Afrikaners moved into an area outside of the Cape known as the Karoo where they established large families, carved out huge farms, and practiced mixed farming and herding. Warfare against the Khoisan escalated to genocide, and commando raids were launched against other African peoples inhabiting the area. During the nineteenth century, powerful African nations emerged as Shaka amalgamated more than one million people into the Zulu nation and set off the *mfecane,* or the crushing and scattering of peoples. Drought and famine also caused hundreds of thousands of Bantu-speaking people to migrate into the southern and western regions. As populations grew and trade expanded, competition for land and trade routes increased. Consequently, warfare between the Afrikaner and African peoples intensified.

The complex social and political scene was compounded by the British when they seized control of the Cape, instituted taxes, regulated trade, and attempted to abolish slavery. Unwilling to submit to the British, the Boers set off on the Great Trek and migrated into the interior where they set up small Afrikaner republics and clashed with various African people on the frontier. Pressure to seize and control land escalated as diamonds and gold were discovered, and violent bloodshed continued throughout the nineteenth century as Afrikaner, British, and African forces vied for power.

In 1906, Britain relinquished the parliamentary government to the South African republics and enfranchised only the white South Africans; in 1910, the Cape Colony, Natal, the Transvaal, and the Orange Free State formed the first Union of South Africa. Shortly thereafter, in 1913, the Afrikaner and British citizens instituted the Natives Land Act, which limited African's ownership of land to 7 percent of the country, located in native reserves also known as Bantustans or homelands.

The second plot in *Time of the Butcherbird* picks up the theme of forced relocation and focuses on the mass removal of black South Africans. The people of the Karoo who have inhabited the area for centuries are forcibly relocated to a barren and impoverished Bantustan in order to make room for an Afrikaner mining project. Although Hlangeni, the headman, sends representatives to reason with the local officials, the mass removal is enforced under the Group Areas Act. Believing he has no choice, the once-proud

Hlangeni clings to the power bestowed upon him by the apartheid regime and acquiesces. In contrast, his militant sister, Mma-Tau, organizes the people to defend themselves and their ancestral lands. She defies the officials who attempt to herd the people onto Hannes Meulen's farm trucks and refuses to be transported to the railway line; instead, she leads the people into the mountains to form a resistance movement. Mma-Tau invites Shilling Murile to join them, for she believes that personal vengeance can provide powerful energy within the struggle; she also knows that individual retribution will never result in freedom and justice for the people of South Africa.

This section of the novel refers to the principles of apartheid, which were put into place in 1948 by the Afrikaner National Party. The political ideology of apartheid, or the separate development of races, was systematically instituted in the early 1950s through numerous laws such as the Population Registration Act, which classified people into one of four racial categories: White, Colored, Indian Asian, or African. The Group Areas Act declared that each racial group must live in its own area, and the reinstated Pass Laws required every African adult to carry a passbook including personal information, an identification number, details of employment, and fingerprints. Other oppressive laws included the Suppression of Communism Act, which declared the Communist Party illegal and allowed the government to outlaw any person connected with communism; the Immorality Act, which prohibited sexual relations between whites and members of other races; the Bantu Education Act, which limited education for Africans; and the Bantu Authorities Act, which established local chiefs as the agents of the apartheid government in the Bantustans.

As the personal and societal conflicts between the Afrikaners and Africans unfold in *Time of the Butcherbird*, the third plot illustrates the hypocrisy of the British community. As Edgar Stopes travels the country selling items to small shops in rural areas, he courts a young, frivolous woman named Maisie Barends who works in her parents' shop on the edge of a black community. Although Stopes and the Barends family are English, they are like the Afrikaners because they exploit and disdain the African people. Furthermore, Stopes enjoys the privileges of the Afrikaners by virtue of his skin color, as he simultaneously disdains and criticizes this oppressive community. Stopes marries Maisie, but he is basically unhappy. Likewise, Maisie is essentially bored with Stopes; she dedicates her life to music, movies, and extramarital love affairs and believes herself to be superior to the African people simply because she is white.

As the hypocritical Stopes travels the country exploiting the Africans, and as Hannes Meulen and his community implement the grand land design of apartheid, the bells of the great Dutch Reformed Church call the Afrikaners to prayer. Stopes is a guest at the Afrikaner hotel across the street from the church, and Hannes Meulen is attending the prayer service. The Afrikaner people have gathered to pray for rain. In a thundering sermon, the preacher, Dominee Visser, hammers out the basic tenets of God's covenant with the Afrikaner people and reminds the congregation that the heathen have been delivered to them by Almighty God. He explains that the people have sinned grievously by polluting pure Afrikaner blood with the blood of other races, and the devastating drought is God's punishment for their failure to uphold the rigid racial system.

The three sets of characters and the three plots converge as Shilling Murile exacts his revenge upon Hannes Meulen. Upon his release from jail, Shilling enters the Meulen family's farmhouse and finds only the dying Oupa, who is hallucinating about his battles with the Khoisan in the early days. Shilling removes one of Hannes' new automatic shotguns and walks to town where he finds Hannes in the hotel across the street from the Dutch Reformed Church. Edgar Stopes, a regular at the hotel, is exchanging greetings with Hannes as Shilling appears. Shilling aims silently, pulls the trigger, and blows off Hannes Meulen's head. The second shot kills the astounded Edgar Stopes. Having avenged himself personally, Shilling slings Hannes' shotgun over his shoulder and joins the shepherd Madonele in the bush. Together they head up into the mountain to join Mma-Tau and arm the resistance movement of the people of the Karoo.

The end of the novel calls the disenfranchised people of South Africa to organized resistance. Historically, this resistance was implemented by the African National Congress (ANC), which was established in 1912. In 1944, four years before the Afrikaner National Party came into power, the ANC Youth League was founded by Oliver Tambo, Walter Sisulu, and Nelson Mandela. These young leaders instituted a program of civil disobedience against the pass system and other laws. In 1950, the ANC called a general strike to protest the Group Areas Act, and all anti-apartheid activity was subsequently outlawed by the government.

In 1952, the ANC and its allies launched the Defiance Campaign in which over 8,000 people were arrested. Other groups such as the South African Indian Congress, the South African Colored People's Organization, and the South African Congress of Trade Unions worked with the ANC to convene the Congress of the People and adopt the Freedom Charter. In 1956, South African women launched their own campaign against the pass laws, and the government accused 156 activists, including Alex La Guma, in the famous treason trial which was to last for four years.

The Pan Africanist Congress (PAC) was established in 1959 and protested the pass laws, and in 1960, sixty-nine Africans demonstrating peacefully against the hated pass law system were killed by police in the brutal Sharpeville Massacre. In the same year, thirty Africans were shot in the Pondoland Massacre, and the country erupted in anger and violence. The government declared a state of emergency, and the ANC and the PAC were banned. Finally, in 1961 the ANC organized a military unit known as Umkhonto We Sizwe, the Spear of the Nation. At the 1964 Rivonia Trial, Nelson Mandela, Walter Sisulu, and others were accused of sabotage and sentenced to life imprisonment on the desolate Robben Island off the coast of Cape Town. Nevertheless, the resistance movement continued. Hundreds of students were killed in Soweto in 1976 while demonstrating against the use of the Afrikaans language in the schools, and the following year, Steve Biko, president of the South African Students Organization, was murdered while in police custody. Again the nation exploded in anger. The government responded by banning seventeen black consciousness organizations, and the United Nations Security Council imposed a mandatory embargo on the supply of arms to South Africa. The government again declared a general state of emergency in the blood-soaked South Africa.

Literary Techniques in Time of the Butcherbird

Initially, it is crucial for students to understand that *Time of the Butcherbird* consists of three distinct plots with three distinct casts of characters. These plots are woven together through the main conflict between the African people and the Afrikaners and converge in the final denouement. However, the author moves from one plot to another throughout the novel without indicating the shifts in chapter titles or subtitles.

The use of the environment to reflect the major conflicts in the novel, set the mood, and reveal the feelings of the characters is one of Alex La Guma's characteristic literary techniques. For example, as the novel opens, the remote, barren location where Hlangeni and his forlorn followers are dumped like "odds and ends" of discarded furniture is described as "flat and featureless," and the dust kicked up by the government trucks hangs in the sky and smudges the blistering afternoon sun that appears as a "daub of white-hot metal through the moving haze" (p. 1). The dust settles on the sullen faces of the African people, "powdering them grey and settling in the perspiring lines around mouths and in the eye sockets," giving them "the look of scarecrows left behind, abandoned in this place" (p. 1). The Karoo itself reflects the strong and bold outlines of the story, for the Karoo, a dry, semi-desert, harsh environment, stands as a racial divide between the extremely conservative Afrikaners and the people of the Karoo. Overall, the general despair of the natural setting heightens the human despair experienced by the characters. For example, throughout the novel, the drought symbolizes the hopeless life of apartheid South Africa not only for the displaced indigenous people, but for all South Africa's people. However, nature also provides the image of the butcherbird—one who naturally hunts sorcerers and impales insects—as a symbol of action and retribution.

Points to Ponder

As students study the characters, the tensions of life within South Africa become evident. For example, the two main characters, Shilling Murile and Hannes Meulen, are pitted against one another. How does each character personify the history, attitude, and perceived rights of his community? Is Shilling justified in avenging his brother? Are both Shilling and Hannes victims of the society into which they were born, or are they responsible for creating the society in which they live? Who are the basic characters in the African, Afrikaner, and English communities, and how do these characters relate to one another?

In many ways, the three women in the novel also personify characteristics of their respective communities. How does Mma-Tau of the people of the Karoo compare and contrast with Rina Steen of the Afrikaner community? How do both of these women compare with Maisie Stopes of the British community? Are these women right or wrong in their convictions? How do these women compare with their men? Are they also victims of a violent and unjust society which they helped to create? How do you explain the stark roles the author has assigned to his characters? Are the characters stereotypes? Why would an author who had dedicated himself to a multiracial, anti-apartheid campaign with the Communist Party and the ANC depict characters in such black and white terms?

In the overall theme of the novel, Shilling Murile and his family suffer personal injustice at the hands of Hannes Meulen; the community suffers social injustice at the hands of the Afrikaners and British. Neither Shilling nor the community can negotiate the power structure because of the color of their skin. In his individual act of vengeance, Shilling Murile is like the butcherbird, the common name for the black and white fiscal shrike in South Africa. The butcherbird inhabits rural areas and systematically preys on the parasites that live on pigs, sheep, and cattle. According to oral tradition, it is a bird of good omen and a symbol of positive energy in society—energy that destroys negative life-sucking forces such as wizards and sorcerers.

In his revenge, Shilling Murile destroys two bloodsucking ticks—Hannes Meulen and Edgar Stopes; he is then prepared to join Mma-Tau and his people in an organized resistance movement. For Shilling Murile, the time of the butcherbird has finally come in South Africa. Therefore, what is the significance of the title of the novel? Is Shilling Murile right to act as the butcherbird of injustice? How was the butcherbird mentality instrumental in securing freedom for all people in South Africa? Finally, in 1946, a squatter leader named Monagohoa wrote the following:

> The government is beaten,
> Because even the government of England
> could not stop the people from squatting.
>
> The government is like a man who has
> A cornfield which is invaded by birds.
> He chases the birds from one part of the
> field and they alight in another part of the field.
>
> We squatters are the birds.
> The government sends its policeman to chase
> us away and we move off and occupy another field spot.
>
> We shall see whether it is the farmer or
> the birds who get tired first.

How do the birds in this squatter's poem compare with the butcherbird of the novel? What do the birds of Monagohoa's statement indicate about land in South Africa? Historically, how did the white minority, who comprised approximately 13 percent of the South African population during the final years of apartheid, confine the black South Africans, who comprised approximately 80 percent of the population, to less than 13 percent of the land in the country? A more in-depth understanding of land and labor in apartheid South Africa may be helpful in discussing these issues.

Land and Labor in South Africa
As the European settlers systematically wrested the land from the Khoisan, Xhosa, Ndebele, Sotho, Zulu, and other African peoples through centuries of warfare, the South African government continued to squeeze the land out of Africans through legislation and the forced removal and resettlement of peoples. The initial Natives Land Act of 1913 made it illegal for Africans to purchase or lease lands anywhere outside designated reserves or Bantustans, which were dusty parcels of land scattered around the country. The control of land ownership was later extended to all racial groups through the Group Areas Act of 1950. This law declared that people in one racial group who owned land or businesses in areas designated for another racial group must be relocated. The Prevention of Illegal Squatting Act of 1951 carried the land legislation further by forcibly removing Africans from public or privately owned lands to resettlement camps. As a result of these laws, African farmers living outside designated areas were stripped of their livestock and turned off the land their ancestors had farmed for centuries. The great proportion of fertile land was distributed to white South Africans, who were a minority of the population, and a fraction of the land was appropriated for Africans, who made up approximately 80 percent of the population. Some of the Bantustans that were developed include Bophuthatswana, which consisted of seven disconnected parcels of dry land, designated as the homeland of the southern Tswana people; and KwaZulu,

a collection of twenty-five separate pieces of desperately eroded land, designated for the Zulu people. The various African peoples were separated from one another in the Bantustans and encouraged to speak their own indigenous languages; furthermore, under the Bantu Authorities Act, each Bantustan was controlled by local chiefs who were appointed by the South African government.

Other legislation extended land control to the "Colored" and Indian populations and urban areas. The most devastating example is the destruction of the "Colored" settlement known as District Six in Cape Town, which was rezoned for whites and razed to the ground. Like the Africans, the entire "Colored" community was forced to relocate. Furthermore, the Resettlement Act of 1956 dissolved existing property rights of people of mixed background and destroyed long-established African settlements in cities such as Johannesburg. Slums and shantytowns were wiped out, and Africans were forcibly moved into a huge complex of townships to the southwest of the city known as the South Western Townships or Soweto. Furthermore, in many urban areas, African workers were prevented from living with their families in town, and hostels were set up for single men in the townships.

It is estimated that the apartheid government of the National Party forcibly relocated over three million South African people over the years. In many cases, the resettlement schemes moved Africans into areas without water, housing, electricity, or educational facilities and forced them to live on infertile and impoverished land that was impossible to cultivate. Essentially, the homelands and townships acted as reserves of African labor. Through the Pass Laws and amendments to the Bantu Laws, a national labor bureau controlled the movement of all Africans outside the homelands and townships and distributed African labor according to the needs of white employers. In essence, the control of land meant the control of life and labor in South Africa, and the systematic control of land became the kingpin of the grand design of apartheid.

The Author and His Work

Alex La Guma

Alex La Guma was born into a politically conscious family of mixed race in District Six, one of the urban slums on the periphery of Cape Town, on February 20, 1925. His father's parents were of Indonesian and German descent and traveled from Malagasy to the Cape in the nineteenth century; his mother's parents were Dutch, Indonesian, and Scottish and immigrated from Indonesia and Scotland about the same time. James La Guma, Alex La Guma's father, was a political activist who introduced his son to the concepts of freedom and justice. After working in industry, on the farms, and in the diamond mines of southern Africa, James La Guma organized a branch of the Industrial and Commercial Workers Union in South West Africa. He then became the administrative secretary of the union in Cape Town and organized a garment workers' strike in 1924. He also joined the South African Communist Party and was serving on the central committee when the party was banned in 1950. James La Guma was politically active throughout his life. In addition to developing his son's political consciousness, he introduced Alex to literature and encouraged his creative writing.

Alex La Guma attended the Upper Ashley Primary school and then the Trafalagar High School in Cape Town. As a youth, he was dedicated to the spirit of democracy and dreamed of fighting fascism in Spain and Germany. He left high school to work in a furniture warehouse and later a metal box factory, completing high school in the evenings at the Cape Technical College. In 1946, La Guma began his political career and organized a strike for higher wages and better working conditions at the metal box company. He subsequently lost his job, worked as a bookkeeper for various companies, and, as the National Party came into power in 1948, joined the South African Communist Party.

As the apartheid government instituted laws such the Suppression of Communism Act and the Group Areas Act in the early 1950s, La Guma became active in the Defiance Campaign. He served as the chairman of the South African Colored Peoples Organization, which solidified the work of all anti-racist groups under the banner of the African National Congress. At this time, he also married Blanche Herman, a politically conscious nurse and midwife dedicated to working for the poor.

In 1956, Alex La Guma worked with other South African leaders to draw up the Freedom Charter; on December 13th he and 155 other leaders, including Oliver Tambo and Nelson Mandela, were charged with treason and arrested. The famous treason trial dragged on for four years and subjected La Guma to endless harassment by the security police, extended periods of house arrest, imprisonment, and banning. Although he was not permitted to engage in political activity during this time, he worked as a reporter for the liberal Cape Town newspaper *New Age* and published several short stories.

The treason trial ended in 1960, and all the accused were acquitted. In the same year, a defiant but peaceful rally against the passbook system was held in Sharpeville; sixty-nine demonstrators were killed and hundreds were injured by the South African police. In the aftermath of the Sharpeville Massacre, the assassination of Prime Minister Verwoerd was attempted and a state of emergency was declared. All those accused in the treason trial were arrested again, and La Guma was detained at the Roeland Street jail and Worcester prison without trial for seven months. La Guma continued his political activity, however, and in 1961 organized the people of mixed race in Cape Town in a general strike boycotting the national celebration of the apartheid state. La Guma was banned by the government in 1962 and was not allowed to attend public meetings. At the same time, however, Mbari Press in Nigeria published *A Walk in the Night*.

In 1963 La Guma was again detained on suspicion of working with Umkhonto We Sizwe (Spear of the Nation), the underground military movement of the African National Congress, and placed under house arrest for five years. Undaunted, he continued writing. In 1964 Seven Seas Books in East Berlin published *And A Threefold Cord*. La Guma was again detained for promoting the underground work of the banned South African Communist Party. In September of 1966, he and his family were granted permanent exit visas. Rather than serve a second five-year-term of house arrest, the La Gumas emigrated to England.

In London, Alex La Guma worked for a private radio agency where he wrote short radio plays and prepared broadcasts for Africa. In 1967, he published *The Stone Country*, and throughout this period participated in numerous international conferences. He also traveled to Moscow as the guest of the Union of Soviet Writers. In 1971, La Guma edited *Apartheid: A Collection of Writing on South African Racism by South Africans*, and in 1972 Heinemann published *In the Fog of the Seasons' End*.

La Guma's international political and literary activity increased, and in 1976 he served as writer-in-residence at the University of Dar-es-Salaam in Tanzania. In 1977 he became the acting secretary general of the Afro-Asian Writers Association, and in 1978 he published *A Soviet Journey*. At this time, La Guma was appointed the chief representative of the African National Congress (ANC) in the Caribbean with a residence in Havana, Cuba. La Guma continued to combine politics with creative writing and in 1979 published *Time of the Butcherbird*. For the remainder of his life, La Guma directed the work of the African National Congress in the Caribbean; he was in the process of writing another novel tentatively titled *Zone of Fire* when he suffered a fatal heart attack on October 11, 1986. Alex La Guma's death was a tremendous blow for the freedom movement; however, through his creative vision, he has chronicled life in the apartheid state, and his relentless commitment to freedom continues to inspire millions of South Africans to strive for peace and justice in the new republic.

For a comprehensive review of La Guma's life and work, the reader is referred to Cecil Abrahams' text entitled *Alex La Guma* published by Twayne Publishers in Boston in 1985.

Alex La Guma's Work

Alex La Guma's short stories and novels describe the social and economic reality of life for the majority of South Africans under the apartheid regime.

In addition to re-creating the dismal living conditions of Cape Town's slums and sketching ghostly characters doomed to live in poverty, Alex La Guma delves into the individual psyches of oppressors and victims, recreates prison life, describes the underground freedom struggle, and explores issues such as the forced removal of people from ancestral lands. The author skillfully depicts the effect of the environment on the people of South Africa and illustrates the movement from complacency to resistance among the oppressed.

Alex La Guma's short stories have been translated into fifteen languages and published in a variety of anthologies and journals such as *Black Orpheus* and *The New African*. Many of his stories such as "Nocturne" and "Slipper Satin" focus on the life of the Cape community and depict race relations between people of mixed race and other racial groups. Other stories such as "Out of Darkness" and "Tattoo Marks and Nails" reflect prison life and reveal the abysmal conditions of South African prisons.

Many of the themes explored in the stories are reflected in La Guma's first short novel, *A Walk in the Night*, published in 1962. This novel illustrates the Cape community's inability to react to the racist oppression of the South African regime, describes life in the notorious slum known as District Six, and depicts characters walking aimlessly in the dark night of apartheid. District Six is a filthy, squalid ghetto of decrepit tin shanties, teeming with impoverished people surrounded by crime, violence, illicit sex, liquor, drugs, and gambling. The slum is home to Michael Adonis and Willieboy. Michael Adonis is an eager worker who is mistreated and insulted in the white workplace. Upon leaving his white employer, Michael wanders through District Six and is invited to drink a glass of port by his neighbor, Uncle Doughty, a feeble old Irishman who was once a great Shakespearean actor. Blurring his memory of the white worker who had insulted him with Uncle Doughty, an angry Michael strikes and unintentionally kills the old man. As he flees the scene, the skollie or local thugs invite Michael to join the underground world of crime. In the meantime the freeloader Willieboy stops by to beg Uncle Doughty for money to buy drugs and is shocked to find him dead. A tenant presumes Willieboy has killed the old man, and the youth's life is instantly transformed into a fugitive's run from the law. Willieboy is stalked like prey by Constable Raalt; he is finally trapped on a rooftop and shot like a helpless animal. Constable Raalt, who represents the police state's law and order, creates a night of horror and deliberately detains the ambulance while Willieboy's life ebbs away. Later he provides the media with a simple report that a hooligan has died in a police van. Throughout the story, the characters are likened explicitly to the ghost of Hamlet's father who is doomed to walk in the night until the crimes of his time are wiped away. La Guma takes his novel's title from the Shakespearean play, for the image of the restless walking characterizes the people of District Six who are doomed to walk in the dark night of evil until they understand and purge the crimes of the apartheid state.

Alex La Guma wrote *And a Threefold Cord* while he was under house arrest in 1963. This novel, published in 1964, continues to focus on the general disintegration of life in the slums of Cape Town, areas which are legally separated from the white suburbs. Windermere, a shanty town of cardboard hovels and rusty tin shacks, huddles under the cold gray rain of the Cape winter and frames the miserable, dreary lives of the poor who live in unsanitary, overcrowded conditions without electricity, sewage, or medical care. The shacks are in various stages of disrepair and collapse, like the lives of their inhabitants, specifically the Pauls family and their neighbors. The Pauls hastily construct a hovel with scavenged materials; however, Ma Pauls is forced to deliver her daughter Caroline early in a neighbor's chicken yard. Dad Pauls dies because he cannot afford medical assistance, and Uncle Ben drinks his life away. In poverty-stricken frustration, one neighbor violently turns on his wife and eleven children; another, Susie Meyers, turns to prostitution. Susie is rejected by a poor, lonely white man who owns a dirty service station on the edge of the slum and then taunts Ronald Pauls as too young and poor to enjoy her favors. Ronald turns on Susie and murders her in a violent frenzy. The people of the slum are like frantic flies drowning in the cesspool of poverty. As their tragic lives unfold, Charlie Pauls, the eldest brother, patiently repairs the leaking roof of the family's shack and gradually becomes aware of the social and economic injustices of the apartheid state; however, he is unable to act. Because the poor are either preoccupied with survival or turn their frustration in upon themselves, they are unable to transform their environment. In order to change society, the strong must save the oppressed from the oppressor instead of exploiting the weak, and individuals must cling to one another, for their problems are shared by all in the community. La Guma implies that in addition to uniting among themselves, the black and mixed-race members of the slum communities must join forces with poor whites as a strong, threefold cord, a lifeline which will pull the exploited out of the cycle of injustice and poverty in South Africa.

The Stone Country was written in 1964 after Alex La Guma spent five months in jail as a political prisoner and during a period of house arrest which lasted for five years. Dedicated to the prisoners of South Africa at the time, the novel is based upon the author's own experience in jail and likens South Africa to a stone prison. The jail is a microcosm of the apartheid state where prisoners are segregated by race. White prisoners enjoy nutritious food, exercise, and recreation while black and mixed-race prisoners often face solitary confinement in the Hole and Isolation Block. These prisoners act as a cheap labor force and lack bare necessities such as good meals and blankets. Furthermore, the white authorities depend upon the strongest prisoners to maintain the system of oppression by controlling and terrorizing the weak. George Adams, a new political prisoner, befriends the Casbah Kid, a sullen youth who has murdered a drunk. George stands up for his rights by requesting a blanket and mat and thereby defies the authority of the hated guard, Fatso. The ape-like prison bully Butcherboy, who serves as Fatso's henchman, attempts to punish George. However, another prisoner, Yusef the Turk, challenges Butcherboy and beats him unmercifully. The pulverized Butcherboy is then silently stabbed to death by the Casbah Kid. Although George Adams succeeds in defying the system, he fails to unite the prisoners in overthrowing their oppressors. The grand design of apartheid has created a jungle in the prison and in the nation where the strong brutalize the weak just as the prison cat torments its mice. As long as the prisoners in the jails and the people in the streets victimize one another, the prison edifice of stone and iron stands as an accurate microcosm of apartheid South Africa—the stone country.

In the Fog of the Seasons' End, published in 1972, details the work of underground freedom fighters in a people's revolution. The resistance movement is made up of ordinary people who become community organizers, political prisoners, and guerrilla fighters—ordinary people who not only challenge the corrupt system but necessarily move the struggle toward armed conflict with the racist regime. The underground agent Beukes travels throughout the country delivering protest pamphlets which will be distributed to the general public by other workers. Throughout his travels, he meets many people such as Beatie Adams and the Bennetts. Beatie Adams is a nanny who understands that she is exploited, but is helplessly resigned to her position in society; Arthur Bennett and his wife, Nelly, wish to contribute to the struggle in some way, but fail to support Beukes because they are afraid of defying the system. These are the people Beukes calls to justice through revolution. Other people, like Elias Tekwane and Isaac, are freedom fighters on the forefront of the struggle. Elias is captured by the security police and mercilessly tortured and murdered in prison because he will not betray the revolution. His death symbolizes resistance to all the principles of apartheid, including the passbook system, the residence laws, the labor laws, and the overwhelming contempt with which the non-white majority is treated by the white minority. The horror of Elias Tekwane's murder at the hands of the South African police confirms the urgency of revolution. When Isaac and his compatriots return to South Africa as guerrilla fighters after receiving military training outside the country, the resistance has moved from peaceful protests to armed struggle. The fog of the various seasons of apartheid is lifting in South Africa, for the oppressed are prepared to meet the violence of their oppressors with military strength.

Time of the Butcherbird, which was published in 1979, reflects Alex La Guma's lifelong struggle for justice and freedom and introduces the theme of cleansing South Africa of the oppressive regime. Overall, his short stories and early novels paint graphic portraits of individuals degraded by their environment in the slums of District Six and the prisons of Cape Town. His later work illustrates a growing awareness among the oppressed and calls the people of South Africa to counter the violence of apartheid through armed resistance and systematic revolution.

Resources

ABRAHAMS, CECIL A. *Alex La Guma.* World Authors Series. Boston: Twayne Publishers, 1985. A comprehensive review of La Guma's life and work.

ABRAHAMS, CECIL A., ed. *Memories of Home.* Trenton, N.J.: Africa World Press, 1991. A tribute to the author and selection of La Guma's lectures and essays.

BALUTANSKY, KATHLEEN M. *The Novels of Alex La Guma: The Representation of a Political Conflict.* Washington D.C.: Three Continents Press, 1990. An insightful analysis of the revolutionary nature of La Guma's work.

BERNSTEIN, HILDA. *The World That Was Ours: The Story of the Rivonia Trial.* London: SA Writers, 1989. A revision of the 1967 account of the Rivonia Trial.

BIGELOW, WILLIAM. *Strangers in Their Own Country: A Curriculum Guide on South Africa.* Trenton, N.J.: Africa World Press, 1985. Curriculum including excerpts from *And a Threefold Cord.*

BRUTUS, DENNIS. *A Simple Lust.* London: Heinemann, 1986. A powerful collection of poems about life in South African jails and exile.

CAMERON, TREWHELLA, ed. *A New Illustrated History of South Africa.* Johannesburg: Southern Book Publishers, 1986. A detailed illustrated historical text.

CHANDRAMOHAN, BALASUBRAMANYAM. *A Study in Trans-Ethnicity in Modern South Africa: The Writings of Alex La Guma, 1925–1985.* Lewiston, N.Y.: Mellen Research University Press, 1992. Analysis of social issues related to ethnicity in La Guma's work.

CHIPASULA, JAMES, and ALIFEYO CHILIVUMBO, eds. *South Africa's Dilemmas in the Post-Apartheid Era.* New York: University Press of America, 1993. A collection of essays by South African scholars analyzing conditions necessary for democracy in post-apartheid South Africa.

DUERDEN, DENNIS, and COSMO PIETERSE, eds. *African Writers Talking,* 91–93. New York: Africana Publishing Corporation, 1972. An interview with Alex La Guma recorded in London in October 1966.

ELLIS, STEPHEN, and TSEPO SECHABA. *Comrades against Apartheid: The ANC and the South African Communist Party in Exile.* Bloomington and Indianapolis: Indiana University Press, and London: James Currey, 1992. Analysis of the Communist influence on liberation in South Africa.

GIKANDI, SIMON. "The Political Novel." In *Reading the African Novel,* 111–148. Portsmouth, N.H.: Heinemann, 1987. An analysis of community, character, and consciousness in Sembene Ousmane's *God's Bits of Wood,* Alex La Guma's *In the Fog of the Season's End,* and Ngugi wa Thiong'o's *Petals of Blood.*

HARRISON, DAVID. *The White Tribe of Africa: South Africa in Perspective.* Johannesburg: Southern Book Publishers, 1987. An historical overview of the Afrikaners' rise to power and struggle to ensure cultural survival; text and illustrations based upon the award-winning BBC television series.

JAN MOHAMED, ABDUL. "Alex La Guma: The Literary and Political Functions of Marginality in the Colonial Situation." Working Papers in African Studies no. 52. Boston University: African Studies Center, 1982. An analysis of La Guma's position in the apartheid state.

MANDELA, NELSON. *Long Walk to Freedom.* New York: Little, Brown and Co., 1995. The autobiography of Nelson Mandela.

————. *The Struggle is My Life.* New York: Pathfinder Press, 1986. A collection of Nelson Mandela's speeches and writing with historical documents and prison accounts.

MATHABANE, MARK. *Kaffir Boy: The True Story of a Black Youth's Coming of Age in Apartheid South Africa.* New York: Penguin Books, 1986. An autobiography of Mark Mathabane and his journey from the ghetto of Alexandria to freedom and success as a tennis star.

MELI, FRANCIS. *South Africa Belongs to Us: A History of the ANC.* Bloomington and Indianapolis: Indiana University Press, 1988. A current, inside analysis of the history of the ANC.

MOORE, GERALD. *Twelve African Writers.* Bloomington: Indiana University Press, 1980. A collection including a chapter on Alex La Guma's life and work.

NDLOVU, DUMA, ed. *Woza Afrika! An Anthology of South African Plays.* New York: George Braziller, 1986. A collection of new South African plays including *Woza Albert!* and *Bopha!* with a foreword by Wole Soyinka.

NEWMAN, KENNETH. *Newman's Birds of Southern Africa.* Cape Town: Southern Book Publishers, 1983. A comprehensive, illustrated encyclopedia of southern African birds with a section on the fiscal shrike, or butcherbird.

NGARA, EMMANUEL. "The Price of Commitment: La Guma's *In the Fog of the Season's End.*" In *Art and Ideology in the African Novel: A Study of the Influence of Marxism on African Writing,* 86–98. London: Heinemann, 1985. An analysis of the novel with an interpretation of the author's articulation of socialist ideology.

ODENDAAL, ANDRE, and ROGER FIELD, eds. *Liberation Chabalala: The World of Alex La Guma.* Bellville, South Africa: Mayibuye Books, 1993. A review of Alex La Guma's work as it reveals the social conditions, politics, and government of South Africa.

OMER-COOPER, J. D. *History of Southern Africa.* Portsmouth, N.H.: Heinemann, 1994. A history of the region with detailed chapters on the *mfecane* and the Great Trek, the discovery of gold and diamonds, the politics of apartheid, and the enclave states of Lesotho, Swaziland, and Botswana.

PETERSEN, KIRSTEN HOLST, and ANNA RUTHERFORD, eds. *On Shifting Sands: New Art and Literature from South Africa.* Portsmouth, N.H.: Heinemann, 1991. A collection of new fiction, poetry, art, photos, and articles from South Africa.

SHILLINGTON, KEVIN. *A History of Southern Africa.* London: Longman Press, 1993. A comprehensive history beginning with the peopling of southern Africa and extending to the twentieth-century challenge to colonialism.

SMITH, ANDREW B., and ROY H. PHEIFFER. *The Khoikhoi at the Cape of Good Hope.* Cape Town: South African Library, 1993. A background on the Khoikhoi with a collection of seventeenth-century drawings depicting the life and habitat of the people.

SMITH, DAVID, ed. *The Apartheid City and Beyond: Urbanization and Social Change in South Africa.* London: Routledge, 1992. A collection of essays focusing on the development of urban life in the major cities of apartheid South Africa.

STUBBS, AELRED, ed. *Steve Biko—I Write What I Like: A Selection of His Writings.* San Francisco: Harper Collins, 1986. A collection of speeches by South Africa's student activist and martyr.

STULTZ, NEWELL. *South Africa as Apartheid Ends: An Annotated Bibliography with Analytical Introductions.* Ann Arbor: Pierian Press, 1993. A useful resource for understanding events developing in post-apartheid South Africa.

THOMPSON, LEONARD. *A History of South Africa.* New Haven: Yale University Press, 1995. A comprehensive history of South Africa including excellent illustrations and an important chapter on the transition period.

YOURGRAU, TUG. *The Song of Jacob Zulu.* New York: Arcade Publishing, 1993; distributed by Little, Brown and Co. A drama reenacting the terror of South African executions through the story of Jacob Zulu.

A Selected Bibliography of Alex La Guma's Work

A Walk in the Night and Other Stories. Ibadan, Nigeria: Mbari, 1962; London: Heinemann, 1967; Evanston, Ill.: Northwestern University Press, 1967.

And a Threefold Cord. Berlin: Seven Seas Books, 1964; London: Kliptown Books, 1988.

The Stone Country. Berlin: Seven Seas Books, 1967; London: Heinemann, 1974.

Apartheid: A Collection of Writings on South African Racism by South Africans. New York: International Publishers, 1971; London: Lawrence and Wishart, 1971.

In the Fog of the Seasons' End. London: Heinemann, 1972; reprint, 1992.

Time of the Butcherbird. London: Heinemann, 1979; reprint, 1986, 1987.

Index

▼▼▼▼▼▼▼